SUMMER
WITH MORRISON

The Early Life and Times of
James Douglas Morrison

A Memoir By
Dennis C. Jakob

All rights reserved. No part of this book may be used or reproduced in any manner whatsoever without written permission of the author and copyright holder, except in the case of brief quotations embodied in articles and reviews.
For information, email us at
Inquiries@IonDrivePublishing.com.

First Printing, 2011, in the USA

Copyright © Dennis C. Jakob, 2011
ISBN 978-0-9817143-8-7

None of this text has ever been published before this 1st edition.

Photo credit the author for the selection of subjective snapshots never before seen.

Cover design and photo editing:
Rain Livengood

Ion Drive Publishing
Los Angeles

http://IonDrivePublishing.com

to
**Mary
Frances
Werbelow**

SUMMER'S ALMOST GONE

A Foreword by **Michael C Ford**

So, then, what you are holding, here, is testimony as to how Dennis Jakob is, by fluke, by friendship, and by circumstance of UCLA film school camaraderie, writing in a way which transmogrifies into a sort of *insider* confidant to Morrison/s fledgling years of cultural anarchy, as well as an investigation of chaos, blood, and madness inherent in his visions of the short circuitry of American political wiring.

It is the core of Morrison's development, as a wordslinger, as a visionary poet-singer as a musician and composer, and, most importantly as a reader, retrospectively reviewed, through these pages.

Along with the *spiritual* trials in concert with those of a more cerebral disposition, you will be an eavesdropper during numerous occasions of these two filmmakers dialoging with each other about the literature and film culture which were chief sources of influence and absolutely inform Jim's vituperative style of, not only poetry, but more specifically, how they were employed in his notorious catalog of song lyrics composed, exclusively, for an American band most of you will remember as *The Doors*.

If you were always interested in learning what enhanced James Douglas Morrison's journey as a literary artist and have only been beleaguered, mainly, by misinformed biographers or cottage industry sycophants, these journal notes will be a welcome addition to your Morrison catalogue.
    Also there were those who never knew him, or only thought they knew him, or too many pretenders who would allow you, wrongly, to see Jim through an outrageous prismatic spy glass with views of excessive rumor, fabrication, innuendo, insinuation, exaggeration and egregious lies.
    Author Dennis C. Jakob's only weapon against all of it is his whole-hearted validation, here, in these pages: a coherent breakdown of the most absolute, imperative and personal truths about Jim Morrison's sources and resources which, certainly, overtime, became fulcrums catapulting him into his uniquely orchestrated fame and idolatry.

- Michael C Ford   © Brain Picnic Productions, 2011

Contents

A Stroll Down Memory Lane 9

The Rooftop 23

Into The Night 32

Monopoly 44

The Sibylline Books 46

The Wanderer and His Shadow 55

The Beaches of Big Sur 62

In The Twilight Zone 69

Homecoming 74

Under the Volcano 78

Death in Venice 88

Aftermath 89

Appendix A 91
   Conversations With Jim Morrison

Photographs of Jim Morrison 149

AUDI IGNIS VOCEM

I have heard the Voice of the Fire

– Thomas Vaughn

A STROLL DOWN MEMORY LANE

The first time I ever laid eyes on Jim Morrison he was as bald as a billiard ball. This was close to the middle of 1964.
 He was working as a student-clerk in the UCLA Theater Arts Library. Anne Schlosser, the librarian, had been given to sympathy for Jim and offered him a job shelving books. He must have weighed, at that time, no more than 140 pounds.
 Anne and I engaged in a little small talk and, when she moved away, I strolled towards the library stacks.. Jim was shelving books. I remembered seeing him in my film classes. I stepped over a short pile of returns, introduced myself, saying I was a friend of Anne's, and he said, "Oh yeah, glad to meet you". He cocked his bald head, smiled faintly, and then said, "Everybody meets everybody else, sooner or later." Then he went on with his work.
 I never allowed myself to figure any reason for his shaved head. I later thought it was a response to his girlfriend's demands. Mary could be very demanding. Especially when Jim got out of line, which may or may not have been that often.
 He was completely bald.
 Somehow that image remains important.
 It crystallizes differences.
 To many he was always the charismatic bad-boy with a lion's mane of falling hair, eventually given over to alcohol, fat, and substance abuse.
 But there were these earlier times, when I knew a different man, completely at variance with those projections and fantasies, the fruit of much earlier fancies. I'm going to tell you of the Jim Morrison I knew.

Today I am an older person, and not much given over to Rock and Roll. My musical taste runs more towards Vivaldi, Mozart, Bruckner and Webern.

But, there was a time, once, when I was not so inclined.

Once I, too, strode the High Road of Adventure with none other than James Douglas Morrison himself. And contributed a fair measure to his career, and a small growth industry that shows no sign of abating. His psychology is long gone, but his topology, that voice, is still with us, though at some point he had given up that voice, grown fat, and said to hell with this noise, boys.

+ + +

Now, it is important to remember from the outset that, at the very instant of our first meeting, Jim and I were both living out of a book. I consciously and he unconsciously, at least at first.

The Public Library is one of the most exhilarating and dangerous institutions existent in our society. Jim and I used it extensively.

As for this book, it was supported in its foundations by two others and it directed the whole course of our lives. What this work is shall become clear later on; suffice it to say that it still, exists, though it is currently not read by many.

What is important now was that first look of his: a complete mask devoid of emotion and a slow, measured tempo of speech. In my first conversation with him, the talk turned to Metempsychosis and its central axiom: that all thought is remembrance – he used the word *anamnesis* – a recollection of what was in the mind. I asked him if he knew Greek. He said he did not but was on very familiar terms with someone who knew Greek better than the Greeks themselves. He said it all with a shy, mysterious smile.

"You know any foreign languages?" he asked.
"No. English. That's it."
"Yeah. Translation is something women are real good at. Everything will come out in English sometime. You'll see. One day the truth will come out and it will all be in English. And it will all be translated by women."

He struck me as being, unlike his fellow students at the Film School, a basically serious character. But how could you ever know this, dear reader? Or what this would portend? You, who were never there. You, who only know him as an icon of sorts, or maybe a sort of frenzied Buddha.

+ + +

I then remembered a story which had circled around the Film Department, which had taken on something of the character of myth. Jim had taken a journey, hitch-hiking, with two other members of the Department, Felix Venable, and Phil O'leno. The venerable Venable. I remember him well: alcoholic, temporarily crippled, sporting a right leg prominently plastered in a cast up to his hip. He is now safely dead. Phil lives on, I'm told, and after abandoning film altogether, became a carpenter in Mendocino, California, an area, at the time, given over to New Age free love and bathing. It was rumored he is quite an expert at building coffins.

But the journey... the journey was interesting.

These three had set out from Los Angeles at Morrison's instigation, and hitch-hiked into the vast regions of the American Southwest, in pursuit of the *magic mushroom* They'd intended to become initiates of a Peyote cult and become, eventually, hopefully... Adepts.

This is less crazy than it sounds.

Robert Graves himself ate the Mushroom. And, he claimed, so did the ancient Greeks.

I had a faint knowledge of things Greek myself and I knew, for example, of the Eleusinian mysteries, which involved a sudden plunge into a brilliant light out of the depths of darkest night, preceded by the drinking of potion. I knew, just barely, that there was a connection between those Mysteries and an even more ancient cult which had its derivation from Thrace.

That Oriental cult was called *Orphism* and, at this distance, it is hardly possible to remember what I knew or did not know, exactly. What struck me as interesting was that this journey to Peyote was a kind of re-statement of a very old, mythical journey. The journey by Greek Pilgrims to Eleusis. And that it was an attempt at an American variant of the ancient Hellenic spirit.

Now, what actually happened between these three "on the road," is a matter for conjecture. What we do know is that they eventually got as far as the middle of the Arizona desert, without knowing exactly where they were headed, and were promptly set upon by a band of redneck marauders who beat the hell out of them. Shocked into some degree of sensibility, they began the trek home. What was curious was the fact that, after obtaining one short ride, they were set upon a second time, by the same rednecks who promptly beat the living daylights out of them, yet again!

Eventually, they returned to Los Angeles, never having entered the fabled land of El Dorado. What counted, however, was the attempt itself and its nature initiated by Morrison himself, which revealed, very early on, his interest in the classical world. This incident recalls something that Morrison read once: the fragmentary remains of the pre-Socratic philosophers, specifically where Heraclitus refers to the mysteries of the *night ramblers:* magicians, bacchantes, maenads and mystics in *Fragment 14*. He was thoroughly at home here, without knowing a single word of Greek. He was, however, quite familiar with the word, *mysteries,* which gave a clue to his curiously reserved demeanor: that is, his face devoid of any hint of violence and emotion, resembling the demeanor of Alexander the Great. He was aware that the word meant not simply a cult, but a cult that was secret, clandestine, not open to the *vox populi* and only accessible to the initiated. The *Adept*.

What is important to realize is this: that long before Mr. Carlos Castaneda arrived at his clever inventions, Jim Morrison had embarked on similar cult action.

+ + +

The next time I saw him he wasn't lugging library books into the stacks. He was sitting quietly with his girlfriend Mary in one of the Film School screening rooms: Bungalow 3-K7. This class was conducted by a character named Brocow, who achieved eternal fame by inventing a little metal rod for an editing machine called the *Moviola*: a rod which prevented the film loop of a work print from buckling back on itself and tearing up it's sprocket holes.

For the most part, such were the powers of invention that belonged to the UCLA Motion Picture faculty.

With a few important exceptions.

First there was the tall, gaunt figure of a man named Arthur Dewitt Ripley: six foot five, sporting a pair of absolutely black wrap-around shades. This was the man whom Andrew Sarris once called "One of the most bizarre and mysterious silhouettes in the American cinema." He was mysterious to Sarris, but not to me.

Morrison had heard of him, but Ripley died before they had a chance to meet. So Jim asked me about him.

Ripley was a man of great emotion and great personal beliefs. And while he had witnessed great disappointment and tragedy in his own life, he never betrayed the slightest cynicism or despair toward any of his students. He believed that the Motion Picture was an Art that could be ranked with the highest examples of any other form, and he said as much on several public occasions.

I told Jim that we had only one requirement in Ripley's Beginning Direction course: to write out in our own hand Joseph Conrad's preface to *The Nigger of Narcissus*.

"I don't know it," Jim said. "But I know *The Heart of Darkness* by heart."

So I read the preface to Jim.

"That's really interesting," he said. "You know, that might be the whole ball of wax right there. But do you think anybody could live up to this?"

"I don't know, Jim," I replied. "But I would make one change in that piece. It's the ending. Instead of *eternal rest* I think I would change this to *eternal activity*."

"That's what Nietzsche would have done," Jim said.

"Did you know that Ripley was the master of the retrospect?" I queried quietly.

"You mean like a flashback?" Jim asked.

"No. I mean a retrospect," I said. "A flashback is neutral. The retrospect takes you back in time through a single person's eyes and ears."

"Tell me more," he said, taking out his new notebook...

"Ripley once discoursed on the idea of actually achieving a double retrospect. You can see it used in John Brahm's *The Locket*. And Ripley himself used it in his *A Voice In The Wind*."

"What was *A Voice In The Wind* all about?" Jim inquired.

"Maybe one of the greatest dark films ever made," I answered. "Ripley shot it in 5 days for less than fifty thousand bucks."

Jim was scribbling now. Notes for further research?

"It was about refugees from Central Europe in 1944, and how they were stuck on a small Caribbean island, and there were murder boats that they were told would take them to America, but they were just killed and dumped into the ocean after all their money was taken."

"Murder boats," Jim said. "Interesting."

"He edited Stroheim's *Foolish Wives* for MGM. He cut it in ten days, in the locked compartment of a private train traveling at a steady 15 miles per hour, so that its arrival would be exactly in time for the start of its New York Premiere. He compressed ten hours into two."

"Christ," Jim said. "I would like to have talked to this man."

The second exception to the rest of the faculty was Dorothy Arzner. She was the only American female director to have worked in the motion picture business between the birth of the sound film and 1942, when she retired. She had edited *The Covered Wagon* by James Cruz and had directed some of the biggest female stars in the history of American cinema of the 1930s.

Ripley said, "She's got a string of hits so big you can't believe it." She worked for Samuel Goldwyn who hired Anna Sten, an actress who was bombing, and Dorothy said, "It's not her, Sam. It's the cat!" Because this European Director who first brought Sten into prominence kept cutting to this beautiful Persian playing on her lap. A real picture maker, Dorothy.

"I've heard of her," Jim said, "But I never took a class from her."

"You should have," I said. "She'd forgotten more about picture making than the rest of the faculty ever knew."

Who he *did* know, from a distance, was the most formidable figure of all: the late Josef Von Sternberg. It was Jim's ambition to do for Von Sternberg what Vladimir Nizhniy had done for Eisenstein with his *Lessons With*

Eisenstein; make a stenographic record of the great man's instructions.

What he got instead was a slightly bent, older man with pure white hair and a face which was, if possible even more of an impassive mask than Morrison's. The place was jammed with people, all waiting for a kind of Second Coming from a living legend who had directed Marlene Dietrich and made her a fabulous star. What they got were many long pauses and few, if any, clues as to what drove the man to create some of the most astonishing films in the history of cinema. Each passing day the Sage's mask grew more and more impenetrable, and less and less was said. He had, unknown to the rest of us, reserved for himself the option to write down what he had to say in his own creative autobiography, *Fun In A Chinese Laundry*. Each time it met the class dwindled until after a month all but a handful of acolytes remained. Morrison was not one of them. However, at that point, I'd become interested.

Apparently, Von Sternberg was at some point going to actually demonstrate some of his lighting techniques on a small school sound stage. It had, however, a fair amount of lighting equipment and a catwalk above the stage upon which the lights could be set. As luck would have it, the demonstration was to be held at the exact time that Paul Newman was scheduled to give a talk. Nearly everybody went to see Newman. Only a faithful few attended. And we were treated to the process of an "alchemical transformation" whereby an ordinary young woman was actually turned into a "Dietrich".

"Curious," I thought aloud, "that Jim is not here."

But as I turned to leave at the end of the demonstration, I saw him in the darkness at the rear of the stage, still scribbling in his notebook. Or I think it was him. I can't be sure.

Later, I recall him saying something about how crudely the eye looked inside itself.

"Use your eyes," he said.

"But is this true of people who go into those peep shows called movie houses you always talk about? Spies on life? Or spies on an artificial life created and canned for their consumption?

"Cinema is a trick of the eye," he said. "Persistence of vision."

"Jim, your ideas about the true origin of cinema coming out of the Balinese shadow play – derived from *Fun In A Chinese Laundry* – may not be correct, after all. It might be the Chinese ideogram: some for pictures, some for sound."

"Maybe it does. You oughta write about it."

"It might even go back to Ancient Egypt – that was a solar religion. All you need is a dark room with a pinhole. Today we call it *'camera obscura'*." [Jim considered that in a section of his work titled, *The Lords*.]

"It was also a country whose religion was a worship of death. Step into film and you step into the grave or a womb."

"Which is it, Jim?"

"Hmmm... That's hard to say at this point," Jim admitted. "Yeah, maybe it was Egyptian after all."

"The lost art of Reversed Images," I said. "Maybe they will translate some hieroglyphics some day that might cast some light on this subject."

"If they do, it will be in English. You can bet on it."

+ + +

One day, waking at dawn after a long night at my editing table and Moviola, I heard a friend skate-boarding in the hallway outside my door. I wandered out and found Jim in another editing room sleepily collapsed over his Moviola. He had been working all night trying to patch together something he had shot that would pass muster with Brocow and at least get a passing grade.

I guess I felt some empathy with the lad. For, by that time, I had developed, through sheer hard work, a pretty considerable talent for the assembling of motion picture images. I saw the effects of his struggle and so said to myself, "What the hell;" strolled in and briefly took over.

What confronted me was a jumbled mass of black and white images which made no sense to me or to anybody else. I didn't think it made any sense to him either. It was composed, in this first assembly, of about 40 separate images. It had, however, one striking theme: the idea of a young man sitting in his room throwing darts at a luscious pinup which, perhaps, was his girlfriend, Mary. Curiously enough, this did not strike me as being misogynistic. Rather, it seemed curiously self-protective. As if that woman, and maybe women in general, had a great effect upon his life and these darts were the means of keeping them at bay.

So, intrigued by this distancing effect, I showed him how, by the simple expedient of eliminating all wasteful pans and the usual assortment of tilts and wobbles and rack focus shots, just concentrating on the essence of this *mysterium,* how much more effective his work would be through simplification.

"You don't want to show everything," I said. Von Sternberg put it somewhat differently when he wrote "The art of Direction is in knowing what to reveal and what to conceal."

I had reduced it all to 9 shots.

He looked it over and nodded. The lesson was not lost on him. But a curious practical sense reasserted itself and an even more curious desire to compromise. "Let's be sensible," he said. "It can't be that short. I've got to pass the course, otherwise I don't get my degree."

I shrugged. "Nine shots is definitive: nine great shots."

"Okay, great!" he murmured. "Did you know that the greatest motion picture ever made is *Anatahan*?"

I had seen *Anatahan*, and I mention this solely because it gave me the first clue to what others later divined about Jim. What some said was his incredible dependence on women. This had a mythic and fatalistic side to it, of course, undreamed of by me. His ideas usually did.

Anatahan was a film Directed by Josef Von Sternberg, who made it in Japan, the last film he would ever make. To me it was a curiously dull and unrewarding experience except for one sequence: where the men are making advances on the one sole woman left on their island, and the look of ecstasy on her face.

Perhaps it was that single sequence that had so impressed Jim.

+ + +

Morrison was a solitary type. Didn't know too many people, didn't go to many places.

In those early days he had chosen to absent himself from either the hype or the sublimity of Hollywood, and it was at that point that I actually wrote him off to as a serious film student.

With one exception.

He gave me an old copy of *Film Culture,* the issue that contained Andrew Sarris' first notes on the Auteur theory.

"They're all going to follow this line," Jim said. "You just wait and see."

I looked inside under Ripley's name and found that Sarris said *the man could not be conceived under a single unifying principle, but it was impossible to overlook him.*

Which he promptly did in his book-length version of that theory, called *The American Cinema, 1928-1968*.

I never forgave him.

Jim interested me again when I found out tha[t] Brocow had publicly denounced him in front of his class as something disreputable: a creature who was, as Mr. B[?] opined, "Opposed to everything this Department stands for."

I was not surprised to hear any of this.

I had been so denounced myself, once. Since what it had sounded like – with some exceptions – was mainly a bunch of has-beens or never-beens on tenure, working as little as possible and generally providing only a minima[l] amount of "instruction".

That Morrison had effectively enraged one of those human particles in this mass of tenured inertia stood, as far as I am personally concerned, to his credit.

Somebody had actually done something. Perhaps life had meaning after all.

But the upshot of it all was that he had to take the same course all over again if he was to graduate and get his B.A., something he had originally promised his parents he would do.

As for myself, the Faculty (i.e. Brocow) gave me an ultimatum: turn my film over to "our" use (it was a film on the American Civil War) and take the M.F.A. exam – or get kicked out.

So, faced with the prospect of losing the film – and realizing that an M.F.A. was merely laughed at by Hollywood – I resolved to take drastic action.

Morrison, lacking much money, was an accomplished book thief.

I decided to put these gifts to good use.

So, one bright day we slipped the work-print and the negative out of the Departmental editing rooms. It was on the last day of the semester; the day when Jim officially got his B.A.

I left the Department and so did he.

We never looked back.

What began, now, was the beginning of a time of Discovery, as we both resolved to burn our respective bridges.

Ahead lay a wide Sargasso Sea of limitless possibilities. But first, before the voyage could begin, the last bridge had to be completely burned for Jim.

He was living at that time in a small apartment on San Vicente Boulevard, right across from the Veterans Administration. This building is gone now, but back then it still had an incinerator. It was then that I first came into contact with Morrison's compulsive notebook-making.

They were wonderful things. "Things I'd seen and heard," as he'd put it. The trick was to jot down the obscure and the mysterious, "especially things that have no meaning". Newspaper clippings played an enormous role, as they were simply pasted in between his own personal scribblings; sometimes poetry, sometimes simply short aphoristic bursts.

I noticed in notebook after notebook, the newspaper stuff was ripped out and pasted in with studied disorder. The lines of association that Morrison cut across were not linear but organic, sometimes slamming ripped-off sections onto one another, sometimes in a kind of run-wave.

Let me give you one example of what he was interested in: the collected works of Charles Fort, especially one called *The Book Of The Damned*.

This was an endless source of fascination for Jim.

Fort's idea that *"We are watched by something or someone"* led Jim to make the following observation in his Senior Thesis for a film class, some of which later became *Notes On Vision*, which, as I say, evolved into *The Lords and the New Creatures*.

> THE LORDS. *Events take place beyond our knowledge or control. Our lives are lived for us. We can only try to enslave others. But gradually,*

special perceptions are being developed. The idea of The Lords *is beginning to form in some minds We should enlist them into bands of perceivers to tour the labyrinth during their mysterious nocturnal appearances. The Lords have secret entrances, and they know disguises. But they give themselves away in minor ways...*

I'm not reading this out the 1971 Simon & Shuster book. I'm reading from the original notes.

However, at this point what is important is to realize that Morrison was about to burn something else other than his bridges.

He was going to burn the notebooks.

Now I am the last person other than himself to set eyes on those notebooks, and I had no objection at the time. I regarded it as a man's right. I remember as he set the fire that I had no qualms, no forebodings, nor do I to this day. He was crossing the Rubicon, as Caesar did; and the pressure of necessity, so visibly felt by both of us, did not prompt me to protest. Only when the last book was about to go into the fire did I stretch out my hand.

"Don't worry," Jim said, misunderstanding my gesture. "I'll just make new ones."

Flipping open the notebook quite at random, I said that I'd like to keep just one page. "Jim, if you don't mind. I just think it might be important to someone, some day. Like revisiting your first report card."

I still have the page somewhere in storage. Unless the gods have turned it into dust. I imagine there are many who would like to take a long slow look at that page.

THE ROOFTOP

I had, at that point, a small room in Venice, California, right above the Kickapoo Logan Company; now gone. It was half a block from the beach. It contained a desk, two chairs, a cheap refrigerator, a hot plate, a bed, and a boosted Moviola. Its window opened out into an adjoining roof and that led to a one-foot wall which was the barrier to yet another roof. For washing, there was a place down at the beach which had a cold shower. The rent was thirty-five dollars a month, a sum impossible to imagine in today's inflationary times. But summer was upon us: clear and golden and beckoning.

"Hell, you can sleep on the roof," I said. "I have a sleeping bag."

So, abandoning everything, including his girlfriend Mary, she who had abandoned him, he moved in with me without a single coin to his name.

It was the beginning of a series of strange and very revealing adventures into the unknown.

Venice was not like it is today. Back then, it was a place, caught in a time warp between the vanished race of Beatniks and the still-to-emerge herd animal called the Hippie.

In those days, the air was warm and delicious, with a cool sea breeze that came directly from the beach into my room. It was a slow time, unhurried, leisurely. In those days we had time for anything. Not like today, when life is full-speed ahead, hurtling all of us and everything else towards whatever the hell?

It was a time when food was cheap. One month my total expenses were just $44, including the rent.

Jim was content, I was content, and that's all that mattered. It was just a time to drift and fall out and read and think and talk. We shared many details of our separate pasts. There wasn't any reason not to be candid. He talked about Mary and how she was adamant about never getting back with him. I remember him saying, "I don't know. I guess she'll find somebody else."

She was working as a go-go dancer at the time up on the Sunset Strip, but he made no attempt to see her. It was to be a fateful split. However, basking in the sun, I saw nothing wrong. Only the sea and the sky untouched by smog. About his "crime" toward her, I felt then that she was too unforgiving, and still do to this very day. What he had done was simply make it with another Mary, a girl friend of the previously mentioned Venable. Somehow Mary had come home at the wrong time. I believe she was working late in the medical office, and found him compromised. She at once broke off with him – he the love of her life – and wouldn't even speak to him; a step that would prove very serious to both of them. I believe all this extreme Puritanism of hers was due to a severe Catholic background – which is ironic in that all this occurred during the period of the "swinging Sixties". She certainly had morals and manners, but later on she went through a number of relationships and even a marriage or two as I recall, and never found what she was looking for, that which she had all the time in the days when Jim was just a student and had no money and when she had supported him. I remember she had found him in an old trailer in Florida and took him out of that environment and made him live decently at her own expense.

Not that she didn't exact a price.

I remember, in addition to the previously mentioned incident involving the shaving of his head, that she had once left him at a traffic circle in Florida, after he had hitch-hiked hundreds of miles to see her, and just drove off.

What she'd really done was to make a circle in that circle and come back to where he was to see what he would do.

She found him weeping for her apparent coldness and remoteness. That time, however, they had found reconciliation.

+ + +

Later on, after he had become the great Rock Star, it was not so easy. She told me once that while she was living in Venice West, she would take long walks on the beach and there would be a lonely, solitary figure following her at a distance.

It was Jim.

Evidently, while he was with his wife, Pamela Susan, he still couldn't forget Mary, even though he once made it quite plain that he had made a commitment to Pam and couldn't go back.

Even so, he kept dogging Mary's footsteps through those lonely walks, perhaps keeping watch on her little two-story apartment.

Hour after hour.

Day by day.

And there was not a thing I could do about it, to help either one of them, though later on, as you will see, I did try.

Jim once talked about her at length.

"She's a really talented artist, ya'know," he began. "She can draw the way I can write poetry. But y'aknow, there's never been a great female painter in the history of art."

I thought of a few contenders, (like Zoe Mozert) but said nothing.

"Like there's never been a great female composer."

Here I was not on firm ground. I'm not a musicologist.

"There *have* been women who were great poets and great novelists, but no composers or visual artists, either. I don't know, but it's some kind of a jinx."

"Do you really think so?" I ventured

"Well, all I know is that talented as Mary is, I think she's going to have a hard time of it, if history is any criteria."

+ + +

One evening as we were sitting on the roof drinking, Jim started reminiscing about his life as a child. He had quite a phenomenal memory, when he wanted to use it. About his childhood, the major sequence of events were as follows: an early memory of the desert in New Mexico, with dead and dying Indians on the highway bleeding – strange for the son of a Naval officer – then a quiet life in Arlington, Virginia.

I never heard much about his mother, Clara, but his thoughts often returned to his father, the Admiral. What I heard about their relationship went something like this: "You know, for a long time when I was a kid I saw my father leave early in the morning in his naval uniform, climb into a limo, then I would go to school. And he'd come back in the evening just like any other Dad, and open his evening paper and put his feet up and read. Mom would get supper ready and we would all go into the dining room and eat. There wasn't anything special about it. I didn't have the faintest idea of who or what he was. Until one day..."

Jim suddenly uncoiled himself and struck a curious kind of pose. "One day, it was on a weekend I think, 'cause he didn't want me to miss school, you see. He said to me the night before, *Jim, you want to take a little boat ride?*. And I looked up from my school book and said, 'Sure Dad'. The next day my Dad put on his uniform and I climbed into the limo with him. I don't remember much about the drive except it took a helluva long time. Until we got to

Chesapeake Bay. There was a pier there, and as soon as we got to the end of it and stepped out of the car, we were immediately surrounded by United States Marines. With guns.

There was a launch at the end of the pier and we all got into it. I wondered where we were going."

He struck another pose and took another drink.

"We went out into the middle of Chesapeake Bay somewhere, and off in the distance I could see a ship. As we got closer and closer, the thing loomed up bigger and bigger until it was the god-damndest biggest ship you ever did see! It was an aircraft carrier. As we got under it, it completely filled my field of vision. There was a gangplank of steps that reached down almost to the water so that when the launch slid up next to it, we just stepped aboard and climbed inside. Right away, when we were inside, we were surrounded by a tight group of Marines. Wherever Dad went there were these Marines, a guard you know, protecting him. It dawned on me that he controlled the whole ship, the sole judge of right and wrong, life and death. I remember we went up on the bridge and I saw him give commands. Real quiet soft voice, but everybody snapped-to and pretty soon I felt that ship tremble and the engines pick up. So Dad took that monster out for a little ride in the middle of the bay. I don't figure we went too far. And then with just a gesture he made, the big ship stopped. I still remember my Dad turning to me with a smile, and he winked and said: *Hey Jim, you want to try a little taaaarget practice?* And I said, 'Sure, Dad'. So, surrounded by these Marines, we went on to the stern, looking out over the water. The Marines were having a little target practice alright. There were these life-sized wooden figures bobbing on the water and they were blasting away at them with riot guns."

He paused now and took another sip. "The targets were images of U.S. Navy sailors."

I didn't say anything. It was in case of Mutiny, I guessed.

"Then somebody brought a box and my Dad lifted me up on it and one of the Marines put this riot gun in my hands and Dad said: *Go ahead, son. See if you can hit one.* So I fired away. I felt this raw sensation of power. Raw masculine power. Then after awhile they took the gun away and the ship returned back to where it had been, where the launch was waiting. And we got into it and went off to the pier and the limo that would take us back to Arlington."

Jim knew that this was his father's way of showing him what was being cut out for him: the continuation of a naval tradition in the Morrison family that went clear back to the Revolutionary War.

What Admiral Morrison did not know until far too late was that instead of producing another Admiral, it was to have very opposite consequences.

It produced a poet.

He was always respectful of his father. Except perhaps, one time.

This little story I will, now, tell is the whole unvarnished truth as he told it to me and perhaps gives a clue to his curiosity.

He once said: "Y' know, one night when everybody had gone to bed, Dad was reading his newspaper and I was up doing my homework. Dad put down his newspaper and said *Jim, how'd you like to go fishing tomorrow?* And I said: 'Sure, Dad.' *Course a man goes fishing has got to get himself some worms.* And I said: 'I guess so.' And he dropped the paper and smiled and said: *Well, why don't you and I get ourselves some worms?* 'Okay, Dad.' So we got up and he got a flashlight and put some kind of deep red plastic over the light. He put a finger to his lips and we very slowly and very quietly crept upstairs to my brother's room. And there was a door. And Dad turned on this real dim light and we very quietly opened the door and went inside." Jim smiled. "Then he took me by the hand and we very quietly approached to where my brother was asleep. And then Dad turned the flashlight on his face. And I saw the worms. Tiny white ones coming out of my brother's nose; and Dad took a pair of tweezers and deftly plucked them out of his nostrils, one by one. After it was over, we left as quietly as we came and went downstairs. Dad returned to his paper just as if nothing had happened and I returned to my homework."

That's what he said. That's what James Douglas Morrison said to me up on my roof.

His father had made one mistake. In projecting his son's future for him, what he really did was to intimidate him. And that was worse than a crime, it was a blunder. You don't intimidate the offspring of two hundred years of military tradition and expect to get away with it.

Jim deeply resented it.

He determined to beat his father for it, beat him in terms of power and glory. An ancient story.

So what Admiral Morrison accomplished in the only military battle of his career that he lost – the fight with his own son – was to set him against that sense of obedience which must first be learned by any naval recruit before he can learn to command. Jim decided to bypass "obedience" in the chemical action of his soul and go to the status of a "command" directly.

Or, as directly as he could.

After all, he did not come from middle class stock. He came from as aristocratic a lineage as American democracy can possess: its military traditions.

Admiral Morrison's mistake was similar to Catiline's: errors in timing: a too-quick parade of power which amounted to gloating when he should have learned to wait.

It lost him a son.

As for his Mother – I remember a conversation had with Jim:

"In our living room, there was this bookcase. Had lot of books in it from the Book of the Month Club that m mother belonged to. And I remember there was this boo there by Thomas Mann called *Doctor Faustus* that I neve read. I didn't pay much attention at first. But a couple c years later I got curious about something..."

Isn't "curiosity" a word that describes fate?

"I found this old Modern Library book there calle *The Basic Writings of Nietzsche*. For some reason it stoo out somehow, maybe because it wasn't one of Mom's Boo of the Month selections. And I started to read It; and couldn't put it down."

Could this have been part of Admiral Morrison' own personal library? After all, Nietzsche did have a lot t say about War; most of it quite controversial.

That inspired a blast of laughter from Morrison.

It was quite clear – and Jim himself later talke about it freely to me – that his father's raw display o carrier power had intimidated him and moved him to th point that he vowed to transcend this power somehow beat his father at his own game. *Power*. What is also clea is that once he read Nietzsche, in that older translation, h had found the means to stand apart from his father an the tradition he represented. Once he read Nietzsche h felt himself godlike, with the same ecstasy as the gods. N longer the artist, he had become a work of art in himsel The most precious marble – man – is here kneaded down and the chisel blows of the Dionysiac World Artist ar accompanied by the cry of the Eleusinian Mysteries: "Fa on your knees, multitudes, do you divine your creator?"

Seen from a certain perspective, it beats an aircraf carrier.

Unknown to either one of us, the perspectives ther were ripe.

All this occurring on my rooftop in Venice West.

Don Quixote and Sancho Panza. Huckleberry Finn and Jim.

In that summer we tasted the scent of freedom, caring nothing whatever for jobs, wages, taxes, cops, cars, schools, churches –

And the military.

"How should I know whether or not we should be in Vietnam?" he said later. "Maybe we do."

He cocked his head and grinned.

"And then, maybe, just maybe, we don't."

INTO THE NIGHT

> *The streets were dark*
> *with something more than night*
> – Raymond Chandler

Nights in Venice that summer were clear and bright. We were free: free to dissolve in that streaming summer. That summer I fed Jim, and even got him some clothes from the Goodwill.

He, on his part, was conducting me on nocturnal tours into the very Halls of Hell – that hell called daily life – so quietly hidden behind the drawn shades of windows along the arteries of darkness. These back alleys were frequented by the Night Ramblers, themselves looking for the angry fix of Ginsberg's *HOWL*, just trying to cop some tincture of speed or grass.

My room in that building was the only one occupied. It was a building of empty offices. There was a key to the downstairs and a key to my room. I made two for Jim and then we were set.

"Well, I guess I'll take a little walk," Jim said. And he left and went out into the night, stalking.

I sat there and got to thinking.

Where did he go?

One night when he said: "Well, I think I'll go out for a little stroll," I resolved to find out.

He went through the doorway and I heard him walk on down that hall. Then I quietly opened the door and I slipped outside behind him.

I could hear his footsteps as he walked down the stairs.

So I tip-toed down the hall and when I heard the downstairs front door close I ran down there as fast as I could.

And I looked outside.

There he was, sauntering down the street, headed for the beach. Now, between where we lived and that beach was a long alley-way that stretched from Pacific Ocean Park down to Washington Boulevard called Speedway.

Well named for those days, I might add.

As I tracked him, he turned right on Speedway, which was only partially lit from dim street lamps. I kept to the shadows. I was a detective tracking a poet on the loose.

And I began to watch Jim begin his spy on life.

This Peeping Tom, surveying all in the nightly circles of hell in Venice West, lurched from shadow to shadow like an assassin in flight. And I lurched along with him.

Suddenly, I saw him pause for a long time, staring at the open window of some apartment house near Brooks Avenue.

I, a shadow, watched a shadow watching a shadow play of two lovers in the dark, silhouettes behind drawn shades.

It was all there, life and maybe death, acted out in the Venetian night.

Jim would climb up on fire escapes and sit for hours, watching, his eyes frozen on the panels of window glass, like picture frames, which contained the passages of many lives.

All the energies and sensations of those picture-panels called windows, seemed to be sucked up into those porous Morrisonian eyes, filling his brain with sensual fluids. I watched him sit mesmerized. No program on Television has ever been more hypnotic. Here was Comedy, Tragedy, and Satyr play all rolled into one big bag of tricks. He was watching the insect life of our tribe with all the fascinated absorption of an ethnobiologist. Finally, as the midnight hour approached during that first night, I saw him uncoil himself and back-track the way he had come.

Oh, how deftly I ran ahead, taking other routes past empty office spaces, dashing up the stairs and across the hall and into my room, switching on the light and, with a book on my lap, looking as if nothing had happened.

He came in.

"Been tom-catting, Jim?" I said.

"You know I have the sack and penis of a twelve year old child," he said quietly.

He walked with great dignity to the window, raising it with all the solemn air of an ancient Sage. Then he stepped out of the room and into the night he loved so well, closing the window behind him.

So began our nightly ritual of the voyeur's art.

Oh, what we witnessed; he, then I, peeping over his shoulder, as it were. There were silent conversations through those windows and loud arguments and violence too, I'm afraid. I remember one night a woman in a rage was beating her husband or lover, slapping him right and left. And he took it, as meek as some husbands out of a Russian novel: probably skunk drunk and guilty of some betrayal. Some of these phantoms sat dazed, watching the dull blue flicker of the TV tube. Others played Mozart and one time, even danced. I think it may have been two lesbian girls.

The City at night. The dark life of our tribe.

I remember him pausing along a stretch of boarded up windows just off Wave Crest Avenue on the way to the boardwalk. He stared at it for a good half hour, his eye next to the wood. After he had gone I went over and saw a tiny peep hole there.

Inside, a short skinny man was balling a huge three hundred pound lady who seemed to envelop him with her flesh.

Then on the second night of our nocturnal ramblings, Jim made his turn toward home and I scurried back, taking up my usual position staring into an open book.

"What's up?" I said, and remembering the story of his father and the flashlight and his sleeping brother with a nose full of worms, said, "Having a go at the lair of the white worm?" And Jim, shy as always, lifted the window, entered the rooftop area; and went wordless into the night. *Sleep as the slain white bull?*

+ + +

A day later, he bypassed the Speedway and not at night. I remember this shocked me at the time, because he was always so nocturnal, like Mary his ex-girlfriend. But also because he had gone out around four o'clock in the bright light of day.

This posed difficulties.

It would be hard to track him in the daylight. Hard to be unseen. But nothing was impossible in those days. He walked up the boardwalk by the beach and I kept to the Speedway, paralleling his course. We walked and we walked. Northward. "Where's he going?" I wondered. "What's this boy up to now?"

He kept on slowly walking until he got to the edge of Pacific Ocean Park. The remains of the old amusement park lay to his left. He turned right and went up past the old telephone exchange, crossed a street and went into the Main street district. This was a place for shops, a shabby place in those days, not upscale like it is today.

"What's he going to do here?" I said to myself. "Buy something? But he hasn't got any money."

He swung to his left and turned north until he came to Ocean Park Boulevard.
And then I knew where he was going.
It was the Public Library.
He walked into the building and disappeared.
Looking around I spied a dumpster next to the library window.
Well, as crazy as it was, I climbed up on it in broad daylight and I peeked inside. I saw our Jim waiting to be served by the librarian there. A second later she lifted a large blue-bound book from a shelf behind the desk and gave it to him to read.
I then waited across the street and, after about an hour, watched him head home.
The next day I paid a visit to that library.
"Could I please see that blue book there," I said pointing to it.
The Librarian looked at me strangely.
"I read them by the color," I said.
She shook her head and gave it to me.
It was the *Oxford Classical Dictionary*.
"Sorry," I said to the Librarian, "it's not the day for blue covers I'm afraid."
She looked at me as if I were crazy.
Yes, crazy like the proverbial fox.
For what was in that book was more seditious and a greater threat to the Republic than *Mein Kampf* and *Das Capital* combined, if they could be combined.
Oh yes, I knew that book. Oxford had done its job all too well.
For what went on between those blue covers was a detailed description of two ancient civilizations so vastly superior to our own as to make an honest man tremble for his country if, in Thomas Jefferson's words, *the Gods are just.*

You out there should remember that Nietzsche was a trained classical philologist. We call them linguists these days. And he came to philosophy through the back door.

"Listen, Jim, it was not for nothing that Jakob Burckhardt, a close friend of Nietzsche's, called their society a "culture" and our industrial society a mere "civilization", what you called "a technocratic form of urbanization". Something that had grown over us, fostered by Pythagoreans who believed that *all was number*."

Jim said: "Tell that to a pregnant woman. She's a living refutation of that proposition."

Jim knew all the objections to his ideas. He said: "I've encountered them before. It comes down to this: did they have flush toilets in those days? Are we going to give up our flush toilets?"

And he sneered.

He was both Populist and Aristocrat at the same time. And I knew he meant it.

See, you out there, this idea of "flush toilets" when it's brought up, that's supposed to end the discussion. Why, without our flush toilets, where would we be? Without our flush toilets disease would multiply. Hygiene must be preserved.

"But that isn't all that's multiplying," Jim said. "What about the growth of populations?"

"Always assuming in an age of dwindling resources and ever increasing mouths to feed," I answered, "always assuming that disease and its death toll don't have a place in the natural order of things."

"Why then," Jim squinted, "from a narrow medical point of view that might well be a consideration. But the breeding goes on and what's to stop it? Certainly not our flush toilets."

But who cares about a seditious book that nobody wants to read?

Morrison cared.

And look what he did.

He wasn't what you might call a "good citizen of the world" but few poets are. Poetry is mostly a subversive act and Jim ascribed to the end of a poem by E. E. Cummings which stated bluntly: *There is some shit I will not eat.*

So Nietzsche had led to Homer and Orpheus and they led inevitably toward the *Oxford Classical Dictionary.*

My mind began racing.

Orpheus, whose music made even rocks move. Perhaps also the great dancers of the Ancient World whose descendents currently whirled at the Whiskey A Go-Go. Who were they? We hardly know at this distance in time. But we do know that Orpheus made his famous descent into the underworld, into that heart of darkness which had claimed Eurydice, by virtue of the power of his song. Jim's Eurydice will come later, found in the whirling vortex of the Sunset Strip, the underworld of the Sixties. And having claimed his Eurydice by the power of his infernal songs the question arises: since both are now dead, who led whom down the path to the real underworld of death itself?

But more of that later.

We must return from this excursion, back to the real nighttime of Venice, California. California dreaming?

Or observing the California nightmare?

This nocturnal tendency found its way into Jim's work.

Returning to our theme at hand, his nocturnal instincts if you will, he wrote:

> You know the Day destroys the Night
> Night divides the Day –

Nonetheless, in the Morrisonian "heart of darkness" there are numerous allusions to this Hesiodic-Orphic cosmology.

+ + +

One night, Morrison turned in another direction: South.

Crossing Windward Avenue past the Post Office on the great traffic circle there, He walked down a side street toward what was left of the once-vast network of the Venice West canals. Strangely enough, Venice had a kind of mist that night – it sometimes gets dewy and moist on a late summer evening. I remember him walking up ahead toward the first bridge that led to the first island there. Suddenly, out of this mist, came the roar of a motorcycle and then a second and a third. They shot over the bridge, these great black machines, past the slowly walking figure of our Jim. Once on the first island he moved silently from house to house, peering inside as the people moved and lived there.

He moved from house to house, till finally I saw him slip down a street to where the backyards were. I saw him walk to a two-story apartment house. I could see a window there on the second floor, with the shadow of a woman behind it. Jim stood under the street lamp for a long, long time, watching the shadow in that window.

I knew the place.

It was where the wife of a friend of mine lived, his ex-wife. I saw Jim studying the place very carefully. Then, after hanging about for some time, Jim turned and walked off back in the direction from which he had come.

Those canals were a dark tellurian place, with trees like cypresses, all overgrown and mossy in spots. There were boats in the lagoon, too, some partially sunken, with the water lapping quietly against them. And, strange to tell, I might have even heard a fish jump as Jim quietly moved through the front yards flanking the dark water, along the broken remains of the sidewalks, towards the bridge that would take us both homeward, safe from the night.

+ + +

Then one night some weeks later, long past the midnight hour, around the Hour of the Wolf, I saw Jim strolling up ahead on the Speedway – when, from the back of beyond, I saw this figure lurching toward us. It was a hatless man in a brown sweater and a short unkempt beard.

And, like I say, he wasn't walking.

I don't know what it was. It was more like the heaving of a ship in a great storm, a kind of spastic St Vitus dance and his right arm would come around and slap himself on his left shoulder like the flagellants in Medieval times. Jim ignored him and went right on walking past him.

And then the figure half-lunged at me!

I was about to step out of the way when he fell right at my feet.

I didn't know what to do. It was all mostly in darkness with just a slant of half-light from a dim street lamp.

He started crawling like those blacks who were crawling around the station in *Heart of Darkness*, headed for a grove of trees to die. I watched him crawl and crawl. He made it across the road and tried to rise, but he wasn't moving toward a grove of trees. I knew where he was going and what he was.

He was a "speed freak" on the Speedway!

Up ahead was a long zigzag of rust-colored metal stairs which led up to the top of an apartment house.

"Where do you want to go?" I said, lifting him up at last.

"Stairs... I... stairs... got to..."

I forgot all about Jim and got this figure on his feet. He was twitching pretty badly now, but I steadied him as we went toward those stairs, going up one step at a time.

"Ta... ta... ta... top floor..." the poor devil managed to get it out.

Finally we got to the top floor.

"What room?" I asked, peering down the length of a darkened hallway. Only a single red light shone there. I swear it was the color of blood.

"Okay... I can... do... it..."

So he made his way inside, almost fell through the open door and disappeared into the gloom.

I never saw him again.

Such were the strange nocturnal creatures of the Venetian night.

+ + +

One day we were sitting in my room and Jim looked up from a book and said: "I don't know yet what I want to do. Do you?"

I was silent, having much on my mind just then.

"Either I write lyrics for Rock and Roll songs," he continued, "or I write cheap paperback novels, like westerns about Billy the Kid."

"Music's not my line, Jim. But I think maybe you ought to try and write the books. They might give you a five hundred dollar advance. Maybe more."

"What do you want to do?"

"Well, I've metamorphosed into writing screenplays."

"Think anybody will read them?"

"Jury's still out."

"The Jury was in a long time ago for you and me. We'll never make films; that business being what it is."

"Never say never again, Jim. Never is a long time. I think you ought to write cheap paperback novels about Billy the Kid. Ya'know, Jim, seriously, I once wrote a four hundred page novel about an archaeologist dying slowly by the ruins of the largest colonial mansion in America. It got me Third Place in the Samuel Goldwyn contest. While it hasn't yet been published, I did get an agent from it. And from that day forth, the word *cheap* is not somethin towards which I care to devote myself."

"You worked for Roger Corman, didn't you?"

"Yep. Guilty as charged. But only as a film worke Not as a film maker or a novelist."

"You know, Dennis, I saw that guy once down i Newport Beach. He was in his bathing trunks and he wa playing volley ball."

I nodded.

"He looked like some kind of a kid to me. A clear case of arrested development. He seemed fixated on th ball."

"Well, Francis Coppola says he's the only gu around who will give us a break. Maybe help us mak some films. Though I must say this appears to be mos unlikely, considering how I value my own work."

"Hmmmm," mused Jim; "Well, all I can say is watch him play volleyball. See how he handles his ow ball."

"Well now, that's a mighty funny thing," I said, an it was. "Because you might get a chance to meet him u close once more. I've been invited over to Coppola's t look at his new A-frame. I think I'll invite you along, an Joe Hanwright, too."

"That's the guy who plays a soldier in your civil wa film, right?"

"Yeah. That's right."

"Good actor."

"You know, Jim, we'll probably have drinks an play Monopoly."

"I've never been beaten at Monopoly," Jim sai solemnly.

"Never? Never say never," I cautioned him, again.

"Never."

"Well, both Francis and Roger are big mone players in life."

"I don't care. Monopoly's my game and I've never lost at it since I started playing as a kid."

"Well, Jim. You know what James Joyce said: 'Beware of what you want in youth, else you might obtain it in middle age.'"

"I'll never live to be thirty," Jim said.

MONOPOLY

So we climbed into my green Ford station wagon and drove across to Mandeville Canyon, I think it was, a winding road at any rate, up from Sunset Boulevard. We turned right and we turned left and made a turn at a crossroads and went up a hill and turned again, and there it was.
 A big A-frame cantilevered out from the side of a hill.
 The Francis Coppola that answered that door was not what he looks like today. Much thinner, beardless nevertheless he exuded the confidence and success of a young hot-shot screenwriter, which he was. Then, as now he was a good host, and we were at once treated to drinks.
 "Has Joe arrived?"
 "Not yet."
 We went downstairs and explored the house with its great vaulted ceiling, and sipped our drinks.
 Finally, the Minor Mogul, Corman, arrived. He who some have called "King of the B's." There he was, as lean as a rapier.
 Roger Corman himself.
 Jim said very little. He just sat nursing his drink, his face a mask of inscrutability, watching everyone and everything. He had sampled everything in Francis medicine cabinet and was quite content.
 Soon enough, Joe Hanwright arrived, a not unimposing presence himself. Until I was to know Francis better, I had always thought he and Morrison were the greatest natural movie actors I had ever seen.
 Joe got his drink and his tour of the A-frame and we sat down to chat. At one point, I don't remember who it

was, it might have been Morrison himself, said, "Well, why don't we get up a game of Monopoly?"

And Francis, who loved games of all kinds, got out the board and we went at it. With astounding results.

Corman bombed out early. I think it took him about twenty minutes. And not much later, Francis met the same fate.

That left the three of us, myself, Joe and Jim.

I hung in there for awhile, but eventually, I, too, was forced out.

But as I sat down with my drink in my hand, I thought about the two money-moguls who had bombed out so quickly, though they had played with a will. They knew how to obtain money – but did they know how to handle it? That was the question. And a game, how it's played, and who plays it, can reveal, under certain circumstances, everything about the players.

So we went into the kitchen and brought out some food and drank some more. Francis told us he was thinking about leaving Los Angeles and forming a production company of his own up in San Francisco, an old dream of his. I remember Corman laughing and looking strangely at him. If he were making so much money down here as a screenwriter – why did he want to leave?

Time passed. A good deal of time.

From time to time, Francis would look into the next room to see how this epic game was progressing. I myself retreated there, silently watching. One hour passed. Two.

And then the break.

Joe and Jim entered the living room.

"See?" Jim said. "I never lose at Monopoly."

Coppola was impressed.

"It's his character," I said, toasting the victor. "Here's to character."

And that is how it was, thus far in my Confidential Report to you out there.

THE SIBYLLINE BOOKS

Now it has been established by others that one of Jim's sacred books was Nietzsche's *Birth of Tragedy in the Spirit of Music*. And, as I'd previously indicated, his second choice was the *Oxford Classical Dictionary*.

It was time for me to provide the third.

Mine was given to me in High School by a Swiss refugee in Pasadena who later became a Professor of Comparative Literature.

I forget the date of my transmission to Morrison but I do remember how it all started. It was in a conversation concerning William Faulkner.

"You know, I hitched out to Mississippi once," Jim said, "when I was in High School. Started in Clearwater Florida and made it to Oxford, Mississippi. Found Faulkner in the town square, near the Courthouse. I recognized him right away from the photographs. Small man, with gray and white hair. Wearing this hat and smoking a pipe. He had a cane, too. I just watched him sitting there with some of his cronies, talking and smoking."

I nodded, waiting.

"Then he got up," Jim said, "and walked across the Court house square and I never saw him again."

"Didn't talk to him?"

"Naw."

"Don't you think that was a great moment lost?"

"Hey," he said, "Everything's good."

Now, this idea that "everything is good" was one of Jim's favorite refrains. It would appear like some sort of eruption, now and again, a sort of mantra, a leitmotif of the spirit, if you could call it that. I didn't know what to make of it, usually, but I was really tired of it. .

"That's all you ever say is 'everything is good'. That notion has been definitively refuted by Alexander Woollcott, who said: 'Everything good in the world is either immoral, illegal or fattening.'"

Jim raised his head.

"Who is Alexander Woollcott?"

"Why Jim, don't you know that Alexander Woollcott just happens to be the man who wrote the preface to the greatest biography in the 20th century?"

"What book is that?"

I reached deftly forward and plucked it from my shelf.

"*Twelve Against the Gods* by William Bolitho."

Jim's face was a mask, but he was listening.

"And who is William Bolitho?" I began. "An adept of Nietzsche's. Now if Emerson is to be believed there is properly no history, only biography. And these twelve biographies are the product of a disciple of Nietzsche's who used them to define the nature of Adventure itself. In fact it is subtitled *The Story of Adventure*".

I opened the book and began to read.

"'Assembled in this volume are a dozen lives by a latter-day Plutarch...'" here I saw Jim raise his head slightly, "'...who, by the chance of his boyhood, by the bent of his mind and, finally, by that special aloofness which characterizes all men who have already been to the end of the world and looked over the wall, was more of an outsider than any mere Boetian could ever have been... It was Bolitho's whim to write brief biographies of the following men and women:

        Alexander the Great
        Casanova
        Christopher Columbus
        Mahomet
        Lola Montez

Cagliostro (and Seraphina)
Charles XII of Sweden
Napoleon I
Lucius Sergius Catiline
Napoleon III
Isadora Duncan
Woodrow Wilson

"'The twelve had this in common, that each was an adventurer who for a little moment out of eternity bestrode the world, a dauntless and single-handed challenger, entering the lists against the lords of chance.'"

I paused here a moment, while Jim thought it over, then continued. "What Bolitho relished most in these lives was that moment of vertigo which seizes each adventurer at his highest point. Bolitho always lingered to watch each of his twelve trapped by his own success. It was when the pirates count their booty, he said, that they become mere thieves."

I looked up. "Alexander Woollcott wrote these words in 1941." But I did not close the book just yet. "There's also the Author's Introduction," I said, idly turning the page. "It's worth listening to." So I began to read again.

"'Adventure is the vitaminizing element in histories, both individual and social. But its story is unsuitable for a Sabbath School prize book. Its' adepts...'" (at this point I saw Morrison stir in his chair) "'Its adepts,'" I continued, "'are rarely chaste, or merciful, or even law-abiding at all, and any moral peptonizing, or sugaring of life, takes out the interest, along with the truth, of their lives.'"

Another pause.

"'It is so with all great characters. Their faults are not mud spots, but structural outcroppings of an indivisible piece with their personality. But there is a special reason for the inveterate illegality, or if you prefer wickedness of your true adventurer, which is inherent in the concept of Adventure itself. Adventure is the irreconcilable enemy of law; the adventurer must be unsocial, if not in the deepest sense anti-social, because he is essentially a free individualist... The adventurer is an outlaw. Adventure must start with running away from home.'"

Jim smiled. He had just found a soul mate.

I ceased. We sat apart, indistinct and silent, in the pose of meditating Buddhas. Neither of us moved for a long time.

"Well, whatever Bolitho may say," I said softly, breaking the silence, "the 13th story has yet to be written."

And with that I placed the book on the edge of the desk nearest to Jim. I rose slowly.

"Think I'll stroll about a bit," I said, and quietly left the room.

I maintain to this day that before Jim read that book he was a little like Mister Kurtz in Conrad's *The Heart Of Darkness*, that man of whom Marlowe (the narrator, not the detective) stated bluntly: "I see no method there."

Jim had been without a method, just living and drifting.

Now he had a method: the concept of a trajectory toward a certain way of life.

In a curious way, it almost corresponds to Jim's notion of male sexuality: a long, slow, rhythmic development, then a sharp peak upward. Finally, a sudden and abrupt descent in that terrific display of energy and power called orgasm. I say "almost" because, after all, he said it was true for him.

And of course, this "trajectory" was true of the glorious Twelve, though the graph thus plotted for each one must be considered irregular in timing and in space. It is impossible to calculate a life. Russell and Whitehead and the early Wittgenstein tried to do so and failed, thank our lucky stars.

I remembered the ending to Bolitho's introduction:

What follows is intended, then, a little to elucidate history, more to illustrate it, to honor without hypocrisy the deeds of men and women whose destiny was larger, if not deeper than our own. Above all to shake loose the perception of the adventurer in us, and of us in the adventurer. To appreciate where I am not allowed to admire; neither to warn nor to encourage; in equal veneration for the insatiable spirit of man and for the inexhaustible mystery around him he preys on, depends on, and worships.

Heroes are the soldiers of society, not adventurers. And the story of these adventures could only have been written by a disciple of Friedrich Nietzsche.

I didn't see Jim for the better part of a week as he examined his new "method". Once I peeped out and saw he wasn't there, so I climbed out on that roof and found the book face down on the bed roll, about two-thirds opened. He was reading slowly and carefully. As slowly and as carefully, perhaps, as he had read anything.

A few days later I found Bolitho's book magically in the place where I had first found it, on the shelf.

Jim came in later on for supper and I hefted it playfully and said, "It's not in print any more. Probably forgotten. But there's something in it, don't ya think?"

Jim smiled and pulled a steak out of his pants Hermes the thief.

"Meat," was all his said.

We never discussed the book again.

+ + +

In the days that followed, that long summer, we seemed to drift together, Jim and I, like that other pair of Twain's.

Our Mississippi was the boardwalks and the Speedway. Often we visited Vic the painter and we visited Michael C Ford, another musician and poet.

I remember we visited an ex-mathematician teaching High School named Konrad, who treated us to his plan, drawn up with all the severity of Euclidian geometry, of what procedures to follow if one got a girl "accidentally pregnant". His conclusion: was "control of the woman!"

When we left, Jim shook his head and said, "Someday, that guy will do something remarkable."

I never heard of Konrad again.

Then there was Jose Luis Gonzalez. But his case was unimportant compared with a confrontation he'd had with Jim.

One day, as both he and Jim told me about it, Jose in a fit of Romantic Passion said: "The aim of art is the love of death."

Now Jim was a slender lad, but at once he grabbed Jose in a choke-hold and began strangling him until Jose cried out: "Enough! I give up," thus proving this Romantic fallacy was just that – bullshit.

I personally never saw Jim do a violent thing such as that before but he was certainly capable of it.

As events will show.

+ + +

So then came the time when the idea of forming that notorious quartet, *The Doors,* was first conceived.

In some of his discussions with me he anticipated his future band by creating – *visualizing* is better – a rock duo based on some of the literary works that he had read. Jim and I agreed that a good name would be *The Doors.* I would be the "open" and he would be the "closed" door. It is only partially accurate to say that it was derived from

William Blake's poetry or from the title of Aldous Huxley's book, *The Doors of Perception*.

There was a third even more important source.

And that was Thomas Wolfe, who in *Look Homeward Angel* wrote:

Naked and alone we came into exile. In her dark womb we did not know our mother's face, from the prison of her flesh have we come into the unspeakable and incommunicable prison of this earth.

Which of us has known his brother? Which of us has looked into his father's heart? Which of us have not remained forever prison-pent? Which of us is not forever and alone?

O waste of loss, in the hot mazes, lost, among bright stars on this most weary unbright cinder, lost! Remembering speechlessly we seek the great forgotten language, the lost lane-end into heaven, a stone, a leaf, an unfound door. Where? When?

O lost, and by the wind grieved, ghost, come back again.

Here we have more than one origin of the use of the word "Door" by Jim Morrison.

+ + +

One day we were sitting around my room discussing Faulkner again.

"Did you ever know any black guys?" he asked with an uplifted eyebrow.

"I must say I have, Jim," I said, "they were guys who just kept to themselves in school. I got nothing against them. We just never entered into each other's spaces."

"Neither did I," he said. "See... In the South the mystery is that the black man is God. Only nobody will admit it."

I waited.

"See... When I was in High School I wrote this essay called *The Lynch as Ritual Hunt*. Just stuff I'd seen or heard, mostly by Frazer. You know, the Dying God, The King of the Woods. And The Lynch was like that in the Deep South. There was the forest and the running Black God Faulkner wrote about in a story called *Red Leaves*, and the white mob scared of his sexual power. And they cornered him, and sacrificed him, so that they could go on and live their puny lives the same old way. Why does Huck travel with Jim? Because the black man is king of the forest and the river. He knows arcane lore and many secrets that white people will never know. Yes, the black guy is a kind of adept. Then the mob leader says to the girl who said she'd been raped by the black guy: 'Girl, go on back home. We don't need a witness to this killin'.'"

"But many people still consider the black man inferior," I said.

"They profess to say he's inferior," Jim said. "So what do you attribute to all the hangings and burnings and beatings? If he's so inferior, why bother? It's because "they" are afraid of him. Afraid of the King of the Wood. He knows what they can never know – the lore of the forest. So they kill him from time to time in order to get strength from his dying body. And, of course, to keep the powerful black men down. It's as simple – and as complex as that."

+ + +

Well, things ended as they all must.

I think Jim set it up deliberately. Adventurers are solitary individualists. Jim knew his new book and had a code to live by. And it is unnatural for two individualists to stay together beyond a certain point.

There was nothing acrimonious about it. He just packed himself up with the clothes on his back and a new notebook in which he had been writing his poetry. That poetry which was later to become the incendiary lyrics of many of those hot songs.

Not much later he must have bumped into Ray and Dorothy on the Venice West boardwalk. It might have been that very afternoon. While I was not present, I've been told that their dialogue went much like this:

"How ya been, Jim?"

"Been living here with Dennis, writing poetry."

"Oh yeah? Let's take a look."

Out came the notebook and history began to be made.

You all know the story: Ray says: "Wow! I've never read anything like this before. Why don't we start a rock band and make a million dollars?" After a moment of silence, Ray suggested: "Say, you want to come over to our house and get something to eat?"

"You got any meat?" asked Jim.

+ + +

So the month of June drew to a close.

But in another sense, maybe stranger than before that summer continued on in other ways...

THE WANDERER AND HIS SHADOW

Did he stay with Ray and Dorothy? Perhaps for a while.

He was like some kind of shadow you chase.

He moved about from woman to woman, an old story with our Jim. It has been remarked by others, among them Vic, that painter friend of mine, that Jim's dependency on women was remarkable.

For example:

Remember that scene around the Venice canals? The one where I followed him to that Apartment house? And the lighted window and Jim looking at the woman there as if he were stalking her? Well, later on, I got the rest of it from her.

As I learned it, it was a rainy Venice night in the canals.

I know the waters on these nights, when the tiny drops of rain slipped on the surface like blisters. Jim's light taps on the window had drawn the figure of the woman there, and she looked down and saw him standing in the dissolving cold. She knew who it was. And it took her only a moment to make up her mind

She went down to him and approached this ghostly form still standing there, silent and unmoving.

"Jim?" she said. "C'mon, Jim."

He said nothing.

"Jim. Come inside."

He did not move.

But when she reached out and touched him, he allowed himself to be led inside, where it was warm.

He slumped into a chair without a word.

The woman touched his face, wet with rain. She unbuttoned his drenched shirt and removed it.

"Would you like some supper, Jim?" she said.

"Meat."

She nodded and went to the kitchen alcove as he slowly rose and went into the bedroom. He took off his pants and shoes and lay down against the pillows while she was cooking.

The rain grew louder. She finished, put the food on a tray and brought it in to him.

He ate slowly.

She watched him like a mother caring for her young until he was done, and then she watched him as he reached forward and slowly undid her dress and pulled it down to the floor, where they made, as the saying goes, love. When it was nine by the light of the clock, he rose and went naked into the next room where her books were kept. She saw him searching for the book he knew she had. Found it. Opened it. And began to read.

Long after midnight, long after he had fallen asleep naked in that chair she saw the book in his hand. It was a dog-eared paperback.

It's title: *Only Lovers Left Alive*.

+ + +

He stayed there for a time, languishing by day eroticizing by night.

Jim preferred the company of women and so did I though he certainly had more luck with them than I did. Was his dependency on them, so often observed by others, just a mask? Nietzsche once said: *In the end what a woman wants is a warrior*. Perhaps the women who gravitated toward him were attracted to this quality. Was it all an act to compensate for the fact that in the early days of our friendship he had no money?

Maybe.

However, he did lose the love of his life. Mary, through a careless act of stupidity.

I lost one, too, out of stupidity. Her name doesn't matter.

She's one of the few that returns to haunt my mind. And I'm quite sure it was the same for Jim with Mary. Like *Rosebud,* it was something he lost.

He was comfortable with women and they were comfortable with him. He felt that women as a gender had a future, a greater future perhaps than most men would have. Most men were concerned with the accumulation of empty numbers. Women seemed to resist this impulse.

We both had heard that ugly saying: *Women lack intellect and they lack nobility of mind...*

Jim never believed that and neither did I.

I think it had to do with our basic orientation. Jim was his mother's son. And so was I.

Maybe we knew something then that other men didn't.

Something important.

Like the beginnings of the modern Feminist movement.

"It's gonna change everything," Jim said once. "You'll see someday."

"Maybe," I said. "If so it will lead to things undreamt of."

Jim made visits to Ray and Dorothy and plans were no doubt made. The details are unimportant. What we know is that Ray had a brother with a musical group called *Rick and the Ravens.*

At any rate, there was this club named the Turkey Joint West that they were playing at, and, since Jim had wanted to write songs, he was invited down to come and see what the music business was all about.

Now the story goes that while there, Ray dared him to come up on stage and sing a little. It was his first time on stage.

He grabbed the microphone and let out a primal scream.

Some say he broke the microphone.

A replacement being procured, he began to improvise.

One must have Chaos inside, in order to give birth to a dancing star, says Nietzsche, which I believe our Jim took too literally in my opinion. David Thompson would know more about that.

His star began to climb from that night on.

+ + +

Throughout it all, we never quite lost touch.

As is common knowledge, Ray's brother had one recording session left on his Liberty Records contract, so Ray got some musicians together to cut a "demo". Now a demo is like a show reel for film makers. It's a tease and a hook for future employment. And that demo was cut with Jim singing on it, and I have heard it.

Michael C Ford, our Poet and Musician friend, was living with his lady a few Venice West blocks away on Breeze. So when I received a copy of this demo, I went right over and spun it for Ford.

Oh, the effect of that first demo: a raw sound with a vitality unknown in its day which made the Rolling Stones sound like a bunch of paid *smirkers*! Its very simplicity made it all the more effective: a concept not yet understood by the music business, which seems to overproduce everything. Much of that material made its way onto *The Doors'* first commercial release, with some unfortunate tampering. It was the beginning of Morrison being "interfered with" just as we had been "interfered with" back at UCLA.

But then, it was just raw sound, wild with the raves of heedless ways.

At any rate, Michael C had a tape recorder, and he dubbed a tape off that acetate demo which he still has somewhere, to this very day.

It would be a pleasure to hear it all again one day.

Well, the boys were trying to get something off the ground using this disk as calling card.

It was my idea to give it to my literary agent for him to listen to, with the warning that this was the beginning of something big. He returned it with the comment, "I don't know, it doesn't sound to me much different than anything else out there. But, remember, this isn't my field."

So, regretfully, I returned the demo to Morrison and sadly reported my failure. He seemed to take it all in stride.

He was still an adventurer, wild and free. Bouncing from one lady to another, living as he had been living. We spoke from time to time; and I got the distinct impression that he really didn't talk too much with Ray. In fact, Jim said, "We didn't need to." Now, with that image of the Apollonian/Dionysian duality so firmly in my mind, I could very well see the necessary distance between Ray's cool neat musicology and Jim's wild unlettered (he did not read music), frenzied voice and dance.

But we were not utterly untouched by other human events.

One night Jim came over to my atelier. We were quite alone.

I think we were drinking beer, just talking.

"Did you ever read *Doctor Faustus* by Thomas Mann?" I asked. "It's the story of a composer and it's about the parallels between modern atonal music and the rise of Fascism in Germany."

Jim nodded. "You know, back home, in my Mother's bookcase, I saw that book. It was a Book of the Month club selection. I often looked at it. But for some reason, I never read it."

I got up, retrieving it from one of my bookshelves.

We didn't speak for awhile both gazing at the book upon my lap. What was there to say? The horrors of the

Vietnam War were becoming more and more evident each day. A stupid wasteful thing it was, and there were those like that fool, Buckley, who called it a "holy war" and remain fools and hypocrites to this day. It was a bad war as almost everyone now knows. And a war to be lost.

I passed a hand over the book.

The author was talking to us across a span of many decades.

I never knew if Morrison ever got around to reading that book.

We talked of nothing important the rest of the evening.

+ + +

So time passed.

Jim did not climb trees in pursuit of women, as some would have us believe. He never pursued women in such a manner. He was after something else; his Destiny. He would find ways, sly ways, to make women come to him. He had a shrewd command of female psychology. At this stage, he was not exhibitionistic at all, except on stage. In fact, he was, at this point, exactly the opposite whatever others may say: reserved, quiet, mute, masked. A contemplative type.

He was hardly the freak that popular consumption would have us believe. He was Apollonian in his life, Dionysian on stage. Instead, armed with Bolitho's trajectory, he was aiming at something. Something as far removed from the herd as you can imagine.

He aimed at the heart of American Democracy. He believed in it.

Oh, his voice betrays him in this concern even now. He was a real patriot. His was the voice of the True Democracy of the future, grounded in the Grand Dionysi of the past, in which All was One and One was All.

And, as JDM would say, *It's as simple – and as complex – as that.*

So one day, when he and I had a little money, he came over and said, "You remember the time we were talking about Brando?"

"Yeah. And you said something about *One-Eyed Jacks*. Restoring it, or publishing the original script."

"You know the oddest thing about that film? It was a Western by the sea. An unusual combination of elements," said Morrison

"Those scenes were shot at Pfeifer Beach up in Big Sur," i said. "I know the place."

"You do?"

"You want to... go there?"

THE BEACHES OF BIG SUR

We started out at dusk.

This was to be Jim's first exposure to the beauties and elixirs of Big Sur..

He was to later re-trace our path with Pam.

We followed Route One in that same green station wagon of mine, which still had some life in it. That was a time when gasoline was 22 cents a gallon.

We were emissaries of another generation going to make homages. Or perhaps merely to give vent to that curiosity which seems to be disappearing.

"The King's Highway," Jim said. "This is a mythical journey ya'know." He was staring out the passenger-side window.

Down we went, the Santa Monica palisades a blur and a whirl, passing beach cottages on our left and the tall cliffs on our right.

We would see much bigger cliffs, later on.

It was a charmed life.

"Look out the window." I hollered. "It's Getty's villa."

Jim swiveled around and caught a glimpse of it.

"You ever been to the Getty museum?" (This was before they built the one near Westwood village).

"No. Will they let you in?"

"Right back there in Malibu. Remarkable place Getty built it from the plans of a Roman villa and to exact scale. Never saw it, myself. Houses the Getty collection – paintings and ancient sculpture."

"Getty was a remarkable man," mused Jim..

"Well, he built the villa, Jim. He must have known something."

We drove on.

I remember it as a perfectly clear day. Not a cloud. So beautiful.

We moved on past Topanga Beach and Point Dume near Zuma beach, past the Point Magu lagoon.

"You see that building up on the hill?" I gestured. "That's a monastery. I visited it when I was just a kid."

"The Church always selects those sites with care," Jim said.

We went into Oxnard, then Ventura, where the Pacific Coast Highway merges with the 101, and on to Montecito with its great white homes. Somewhere along the way there was some kind of place with a Santa Claus motif: a reminder of winter in summer.

And then we hit Santa Barbara and I made a gas stop.

"We're going to take a little side excursion, Jim."

We started up again, and at Goleta I turned off onto 154 and took an inland route to Lake Cachuma, recreating an old journey I once made with friends some years back in search of locations for a great old UCLA film, *A Time Out Of War*. It was somewhere near Los Olivos. We never did find them, exactly.

The drive took us into the mountains with some twisting kind of road which dipped into the horse and cattle country of the Santa Ynez Valley.

At Solvang we stopped like any tourists and bought ice-cream and cokes, then turned into a small two-laner that wound its way past hills and farmland back to 101. We did not stop for pea soup but went on past Vandenberg, hoping for a rocket but not seeing one. Jim talked, vaguely, but I forget exactly what he had on his mind. My focus was on driving, my thoughts drifting on ahead, because I knew what we were going towards. He didn't.

"Well, this is it," I said, pointing out Pelican Rock up at Morro Bay. "Some say it starts here. *Big Sur*."

We moved on.

We reached the forest around Cambria. The big pines that rested on the left of a valley into whose heart I've always wished to travel and never have.

We moved on ahead. Abreast of San Simeon, with the huge castle ice-white against the hills, I said, "And others say it starts here: Big Sur."

"So that was Hearst," Jim said dreamily.

Now up past San Simeon, there's the beginning of the Santa Lucia range, and the road suddenly veers up and takes a sharp uphill turn, hard against the flanks of the mountains that fall in a granite cascade all the way down to the sea. There was a gate there once, that the Highway Patrol closes when the road goes out. And I pointed to it and said, "And some say Big Sur begins right here, Jim."

On and on we went, the little car dwarfed by the range and running up beneath the deep blue sky of a clear summer's day. Sometimes we came upon some houses cantilevered off the cliff walls. Jim would talk about language and the discovery of Troy – and then we would move on again in the silence, all except for the motor along the empty reaches, around still but erratic bends, the high walls of our winding way opening out into sea and sky.

Finally we hit the green wall of the big ranges. Trees, trees, millions of trees, massive, immense, running up high; and at their foot, rounding each bend, we chugged on. It was Jim's first encounter with the heights of the redwoods.

Finally, we stopped.

It was a place where a road went down to a cove. And a path went to the right and into the crevice of the mountains, upstream to a place I knew, where I had been many years before. There was a shack up there which I saw as a kind of *Hansel and Gretel* witch's hideaway.

The silence driven away by the stamping of our feet flowed back again from the recesses of the range. The great wall of vegetation, an exuberant and entangled mass of trunks and branches, leaves, boughs, festoons, lightly moving in the spangled sunlight, was like a rioting invasion of soundless life, a rolling wave of plants and trees, piled up, crested, ready to topple over the creek nearby, to sweep every one of us out of our little existences. And it moved not.

When we finally arrived at this deserted shack, it grew still and so dark there it was almost twilight.

Then I took him down to what I called Smuggler's Cove. We took a path down the hillside to a tunnel that reaches out into a slip of water on the backside of a hill facing the sea.

In the old days they had smuggled in Canadian whiskey, I'm told, during the Great Prohibition days. It was a Pirate's Cove, too. And that really suited us.

We sat there on the big rocks and watched the water ebb and flow.

And you could see as far out as... well, it seemed that day you could see to the ends of the earth.

We got up after awhile and left it all and got into the car.

We stopped off at Deetjin's where we had a hard time getting some service, because Jim's hair was getting long. Old man Deetjin was still alive then, and he didn't approve of long hair.

So we went up to Nepenthe and into the bookstore there and I think I bought a postcard. I forget for whom. Did we eat lunch there? Expensive hamburgers! Wandering around over to the cliff-edge, catching the wild world sea view; and the surf crashing in sleeves of silver down below.

Back into my green Ford, and on we went. North.

Up there, on the road called the King's Highway by Jim, you arrive at the highest point of the Big Sur road. It goes downhill from there. At a point mid-way down, off to the left, there is a road and a tiny sign which marks the way to Pfeifer Beach.

It was there that we were headed.

We turned left hugging the cliffs and, meandering through rings of forests, went down the canyon to the acute and abrupt turn at the farm house. It was there that the state road sort of ended and one had to stop and pay ones' dues to the farmer whose land lies betwixt the road and the State Beach.

We paid a dollar then. What it costs now or whether it costs at all and some deal has been struck, I don't know now. I only know the dollar was well spent.

We parked by logs and then, passing through thickets and underbrush... and suddenly –

There we were!

There was the beach as it was in Brando's film.

You could see the big rock and its hole and the surf thundering as it did in Jack Kerouac's mind: *hail-scar, sea surge...*

We walked out there across the beach, crossing tiny stream, and Jim said aloud to the rock hole: "You are our mind, and you are our Sargasso Sea!" Or something to that effect.

We sat on the beach, took off our shirts and let sunrays and the day's summer air flow over our skin.

"Yeah, Brando built this whole village over here," Jim said. "You can see it plain enough."

Then we fell silent for awhile and just listened to the sea's voice and the surf crash in the hollowed out rock there.

I remember there was an old man and a younger man and a young woman with a child in her arms. They were talking and laughing by the running stream splashing their feet in the cold water. They moved toward the big rock and peered within just as we had done, and the younger man – her husband? – raced around on the sands like a young colt.

"Oh, stop it now," the young woman laughed.

I remember she had on a white dress and dark hair

that fell to her waist. And she reminded me of Mary somehow. I guess there hasn't been a month gone by that I haven't remembered her.

But I could feel something coming. Something like an epiphany.

The three of them sat down not far from Jim who still lay on the sand, unmoving.

Then the woman reached out, pulling down part of the front of her dress and exposed a breast to her child, who suckled on it.

She began to sing to herself.

Slowly, Jim sat up.

Then, quite deliberately, he took out a notebook and began writing. What he wrote i do not know.

Pretty soon, we left, got into my green car and roared back up the road to Highway 1.

"What's next?" Jim asked.

"There's this road I know," I said.

It was a county road that most folks don't know about that led off to the right in a sharp hard incline.

Immediately we were surrounded by cows!

"God, I hope the bull isn't lurking around," I said.

The cows drifted off and left us a free road which dipped down past dells and grasslands and then we were in the forest.

Oh, what a forest that was!

All covered over with vines and clinging cobwebs that sparkled in the slants of sunlight... sunlight like it was in a Cathedral. And there was a stream there, too. Paths that I've never taken and always wished I had.

We went on, passing a road that led to a farm house with a sign that warned us, PRIVATE PROPERTY TURN BACK, so we went back to the county road. Until we found it. What I had been looking for.

It was Lawrence Ferlinghetti's cabin.

And Bixby Canyon Bridge.

You may have read about its sinister aspect in *Big*

Sur by Jack Kerouac. There was nothing sinister about that place for me and Jim. Not that day.

"Well, here it is," I said.

"What is?" he questioned

"Ferlinghetti's cabin," I said.

"You mean that place where Kerouac went crazy?"

"The same. And there's the stream and the canyon with its roaring mouth. And – there's the bridge."

We did not intrude on that cabin. There were fences there.

Instead, we rode up to the bridge and stopped and looked around.

Jim looked up the road that poor old Kerouac had trod so many years ago, the hottest writer in America vainly trying to hitch a ride until somebody finally took pity on him and hauled him aboard.

"Let's head back," Jim said.

We went south.

For home.

I know, later on, Jim took his wife to the same spots, but it was I who led him there: I'm glad he thought enough of the experience to share it with her.

IN THE TWILIGHT ZONE

This next part should properly be called: Jim Morrison on the subject of homosexuality.
    I remember that once he told me of the peculiar tension that occurs in a gay bar as the clock approaches 2 a.m. – the legal limit in the State of California for the purchase of alcohol. He described the frantic search to find a partner – or face the prospect of a lonely night. I had wondered then how he, the nocturnal creature that he was, had come upon this information.
    Then one day, Jim said to me and Vic the Painter:
"You ever been to a gay bar?"
We told him that we hadn't.
"It's amazing. All this energy starts to build up slowly around the midnight hour, 'cause the bar has to close soon."
"Amazing."
"You wanna go?" he said.
    Now on the boardwalk in those days there was a bar that was split right down the middle, with gay Males on one side and Lesbians on the other side.
    So Vic and I and Jim went inside.
    There were a lot of men in there milling around on the left hand side, eyeing each other. I just stood there without ordering a drink and watched the "soft parade" of flesh move slowly in circles around itself. I gained nothing from the experience, but I noticed one gray-haired stoutly built character say to a friend. "He's the one I'd like to go home with tonight."
    And he was indicating Morrison.
    Jim made no move toward anybody. He just stood

there as usual with his eyes cast down to the floor and said nothing.

"How far does he want to take this?" I whispered to Vic, nodding at Jim.

"Don't ask me," Vic shrugged.

So after awhile the three of us left. It was not too late, as I recall. The magic hour of 2 a.m. was still far away. All I remember with any degree of vividness was the conspicuous display of white tennis shoes on almost everybody, the symbolism of which escapes me to this very day.

So that is the extent of my knowledge of Jim's "alleged" and furtively whispered knowledge of homosexuality. It may or may not have been extensive. Let others say what they will if they choose. As for myself, I've always taken "deviant" revelations about any and all celebrities with a grain of very low grade salt.

I know from literary history that what others have told me was not the truth at all, but merely *revenge*. Nothing but slander which, for the most part, is the result of a failure to connect.

+ + +

Then there was the time Jim met Sal Mineo.

I remember it was on the Sunset Strip in daylight in some movie theater there. I don't remember how it started, but I do remember Mineo's intense interest in Jim.

Jim just stood there, the same way he did when we were surveying that Venice West gay bar.

Did Mineo know he was being examined in return?

That's an interesting surmise.

There's no question in my mind of his attraction to Morrison's personae. It was very vivid and intense. But Jim as usual wore a mask.

So Mineo invited me over to his elaborate pad just

north of the Strip. It had an Oriental look to it, with water flowing.

Mineo wasn't interested in me nor I in him. I just kept wondering what Mineo was after. It was apparent he wanted some information about Jim. He was curious about Jim's masked demeanor.

"Is it me?" he asked. "Is it because of what I am?"

"No, I don't think so," I replied. "It's just his way. He's always like that."

"Because I would just love to have him over, you know?"

"I'm sure you would. A lot of people like you would."

Mineo just nodded.

He just wanted information. An edge he could use on Jim.

But he never got it from me.

And I never knew Jim to get any closer to Mineo other than this one encounter.

So, you out there, be careful. You know or think you know something. But, unless you're really there, you don't know it at all for sure.

The rest I leave to Diaries and "revelations." What are they to me? I was there. I make my Confidential Report to you out there this way: I never saw him make a homosexual advance towards me or anyone, ever.

I only heard rumors.

And you out there know what I think of them.

It's as simple – and as complex – as that.

As for Jim's wife Pam, she too, was straight. She once mentioned that two of her girl friends had come together in a Lesbian experience. But she wouldn't have any of it.

She completely rejected that kind of experience,

I don't believe she ever changed.

+ + +

As for myself, I got a job shooting and editing the psychedelic montages for a film called *The Trip*. I did not then, nor have I since, taken any Psychedelic drug whatsoever, preferring to take a tip from Josef Von Sternberg and create my own "acid trip" on film. It amused me to hear some of the actors commenting: *Wow, what a great trip it is, man* and *how close you got to it really, man!* I dismissed them from my mind as a band of typical habitués of Barney's Beanery, a place I studiously avoided. But I had my brief moment of fame.

It didn't last very long.

For me things began to go from bad to worse.

Morrison visited me one day, saying: "What you need is to break on through to the other side."

"To the other side from what to what, I'm wondering."

"Through the looking glass," he said. "You need that to pick you up."

"What do you suggest?"

"I think we ought to go down to the Venice hardware store and get some packets of Morning Glory seeds and eat them."

"You mean those little seed packets?"

"Sure. The seed contains the key to open the door."

So, having nothing better to do, we trotted down to the hardware store and bought two packets for cheap. Then took them back up to my place and downed them.

All I got for my trouble was three days of insomnia and a splitting headache. I remember Jim saying: "Go with it, man. Go with it."

I just lay there for three days and three nights without a bit of sleep. I never knew what Jim experienced and he never told me.

The experience bore no relationship whatsoever to the psychedelic montages I had created for *The Trip*.

+ + +

Finally, our excursion into the Morrisonian Twilight Zone, there is this strange tale of horror that Jim told me one day. It appears he knew this guy – one of those denizens of the Deep South who had this "special room" in the back of his garage.

He took Jim inside one day.

In that room were about two dozen very large gallon-sized (or larger) glass jars – the kind they used for sweets in a candy store. As it was explained to me by Morrison, each one had a dead cat inside which had been asphyxiated after having been lured inside by the smell of catnip.

"The expression on those cats faces was remarkable," Jim said. "If somehow they could have freed themselves those cats would have killed that guy."

And if this isn't a scene out of the *Twilight Zone*, I don't know what is.

HOMECOMING

> *There is no trap so deadly*
> *as the one you set for yourself*
>
> – Raymond Chandler
> (*The Long Goodbye*)

Meanwhile, Jim was becoming famous.

First it was at the London Fog and not many weeks later at the Whiskey. I went to see *The Doors* many times and I took some photographs of Morrison and the band on stage.

One I especially remember is an evening in another club called Bito-Lido's, down south of Hollywood Boulevard, at the corner of Ivar & Selma and with a back entrance off of Cosmo Alley: the 1950s home of the commingling of Poetry & jazz experiments. That night Jim gave sensational renditions of *Whiskey Bar* and *Gloria:* the latter of which I claim was more visceral and intense than Van Morrison's original. I mention this only because some people get the idea that Jim and *The Doors* were only their records. Which is not true. They were also their performances. And these exist only in Time and Memory. Mine, amongst others.

I must briefly talk about the state of the *Adventure*.

It is unavoidable. As it has to do with the explication of Morrison's trajectory and precisely when it came to an end, and why he was much more interesting before he was a Rock Star than he ever was afterwards.

As I watched Jim, I saw him change.

Oh, imperceptibly at first. But gradually it became apparent that the trajectory so described by Bolitho was taking its toll.

As long as Jim had Ray as a kind of anchor, and as long as he was free to float about from woman to woman, all was well.

What matters, however, was the precise moment when he ceased to be an Adventurer: that *moment* which became the beginning of his *downgoing*.

It was the exact moment when he signed his contract with Elektra Records.

Now he was bought and paid for. And the Adventure was at an end.

Of course things are not always so pure and simple. This act had its precursors in other acts which gave him away in minor ways.

First, there was the whole idea of joining a group. That is opposed to the idea of the free individualist. Jim began to like the action on the strip. Money came flowing in. And a certain recognition.

And women, too.

When Jim introduced me to Pamela, they were both living up in Laurel Canyon, near the Market. It was a wooden house stuck up against the mountain side. I could smell the marijuana.

I remember, when Pam answered the door, seeing Jim propped in an easy chair focusing on a book. They struck me as suited to one another. We had lunch, as I recall. It was quiet, up there in the canyon. Warm. You could hear the hum of insects. It was like something out of a Raymond Chandler novel. Nothing seemed to come in or go out. Except the music.

I got the sense that what Jim found in Pam was a young woman even more dependent on another person than he himself had ever been. He had always had this strange dependency on women. Now he had found a woman who depended on him.

I remember the time she told me of the great secret happening and sad disaster of her High School life.

She, too, had had an Adventure, once.

First, she was the daughter of the local High School Principal.

She told me that it was like being the daughter of a Minister in the days of the Salem witch trials. She always spoke well of her family. But the fact remains that this condition in life brought out a rebellious streak in her. And, as I recall her telling me, she had a boyfriend of whom her parents didn't approve.

One night he got both of them drunk and smashed a car into somebody's house.

They were both arrested and she was convicted of being Under the Influence.

She was underage and so was remanded to the custody of Juvenile Hall. Once there she had no civil rights. Her parents couldn't get her out because that was the law.

One night, she told me, she and another girl resolved to escape by climbing into the ventilator shafts. They were there for the better part of a week until hunger drove them out.

I remember that she laughed about it, as though remembering something ridiculous, yet disturbing: she was still bitter about the law and all it had tried to do to her.

It's interesting to compare Pam with Mary.

Pam had an Adventure. Pam had broken the law.

Mary was respectable.

Mary obeyed the law. And in some ways Pam stood against it. So Jim stayed with her.

They moved to the beach at Venice West, into a penthouse on top of an apartment building right above the boardwalk, just a few blocks from where I had that rooftop. And I remember him, during that time, saying, "I've been to a lot of places now. But somehow, there's no place quite like Venice." It was a drizzly day in winter. We were on the roof.

Jim was staring down at the beach. Far down below there was a solitary figure.

Was it Mary?

And so in a way what began in Venice West had come full circle.

First, however, we must see just how far he had come, to a point *beyond Good and Evil.*

UNDER THE VOLCANO

I got a clue from Pam herself when, one day, she told m[e] this weird uncomfortable story about how Jim first me[t] her parents.

According to Pam, it was an important day. An[d] things had to be right. Exactly right. Everything in apple pie order. Including Jim himself. Jim was not to pout. Ji[m] was not to slouch. Jim was to be friendly. Jim was t[o] transform into a Victorian gentleman of charm an[d] erudition. Jim was to –

At that moment he leaped up and let out a scream! Then he rushed to the kitchen and came out waving a bi[g] butcher knife.

"No, Jim. No!"

She backed up.

"Evooo! Eeeevooo!" he screamed.

Then he started chasing her around a couch looking, to anyone observing the action, like he was goin[g] to slash her to death.

Then the doorbell rang.

She bolted from the room towards the front doo[r] thinking: "What am I gonna do! They are here – and he'[s] turned crazy!"

She opened the door, and just as she was about t[o] warn them her Mom and Dad breezed right in and starte[d] chatting about Jim.

"Oh, where's Jim? We are looking forward t[o] meeting him."

And they waltzed right into the room where th[e] Monster lurked.

"He was sitting in that chair, just like before," sh[e] said to me.

"As if nothing had happened. And he got up and I introduced him to my parents. And we had dinner and Jim was as pleasant and as respectful as he could be."

"Did you learn anything from this experience?" I asked.

"I guess so," she said. "He's so changeable you know."

Well, it occurred to me that what Mr. Morrison was trying to teach her was that there were times when it was better to let things alone. And to quit playing the role of *housewife* and come back down to earth. But I don't think she ever did.

Come back down to earth.
Until the end.
When they put her in the grave.
Poor lost little girl!

+ + +

At this point I did something I do not ordinarily do. I directly interfered with other people's lives. I knew Mary, Jim's ex-girlfriend. She, too, lived in Venice. All she ever talked about was Jim. In her mind, it was clear that she would always think of herself as *Jim's girl*.

Only she wasn't.

So I arranged a meeting in my Venice West atelier between her and Jim and Pam and myself. I didn't think that Mary would ever get back with him, at least in this lifetime. But I hoped, for her sake, and maybe for his, too, that they could at least have some sort of a relationship as friends, at least speak to one another.

Pam and I left the two of them alone for awhile and she said something I will never forget: "I feel sorry for Mary."

I knew at once what that meant. It meant she was not threatened by the emergence of Mary. That something had long been settled between her and Jim. A relationship deeper than either one of them had ever had before. I'd begun to suspect that something had been settled between the two of them – unbreakable except by death itself.

We stood there under my skylight and talked for awhile. She was looking forward to opening up a dress shop on La Cienega, right around the corner from the Doors office on Santa Monica Boulevard. And, ironically, next to an office space where Mike Anhiman and Frank Liciandro were editing Morrison's film, *Highway*. She said she was going to call her shop *Themis* and it was going to be bankrolled by Jim.

I wished her the best of luck.

But I remembered one time when the three of us, Jim and Pam and myself, were in a car and she put her head on my shoulder. Was this just an unconscious gesture of friendship or was it to inspire a jealous Morrison response?

As I recall the incident, Jim remained inscrutable.

+ + +

So, late in the Sixties when both of us had money came the time to attempt one last Adventure.

It was done in the company of Tony Redman, an old classmate of mine from UCLA Film School.

It was Tony's car and he was in the Neal Cassidy seat behind the wheel.

Tony's car was a shiny black Karmann Ghia, just big enough for the three of us. There was a tiny seat in back, very hard on the buns. Jim and I took turns sitting there because Tony loved to drive and drive fast. Also, I think he wasn't about to turn over the wheel to a pair of unknown qualities like us.

Our destination was going to be South of the Border. San Felipe!

A picturesque fishing village where none of us had ever been.

The journey began quietly and uneventfully, with us following a well-traveled freeway route through Riverside and then past Beaumont and Banning and Palm Springs. At Indio we turned right and went on past Coachella, flanking the western shore of the Salton Sea. The sea looked long and flat, with great reaches of pale blueness which we knew to be due to all that salt. Yes, saltier than the great Ocean we had left behind.

At Brawley, we struck due south toward El Centro. Not far beyond was Calexico. and across the line, Mexicali, and foreign territory.

We crossed the border almost exactly six hours from when we started. Then we headed down Mexico's Route 5 to San Felipe.

Mexico is a strange land. You could feel the *mystery,* even near the border. Everything is a little out of date, a little dilapidated: even the gas stations feel like they are on the verge of being abandoned.

As I recall we had brought some food with us and a full thermos, and going down that road, with the strange bare mountains of the high dark ranges looming to our right, we began to drink.

It was clear sailing that day. Not a cloud in the sky. And nobody seemed to mind the heat in the least.

I remember the radio, though. Tony loved it. It kept up his driving rhythm. It was rock and roll all the way. Up to the point where, down the line, we got those primitive Mexican stations, which seemed to interest Morrison.

I don't know how many hours later we got to the end of the line. Literally. The paved road ended and a dirt track began.

But it was San Felipe. So we backed up and rolled into town without so much as a reservation.

The first stop was to get a motel room and luck was with us. There was a room and we snapped it up at once.

The second stop was the local cantina for some *Cerveza* and for Mexican cigarettes, both, to our pleasure, dark and tasty.

We walked around the little village.

Long open-air sheds with drying fish lay exposed with all their smells and sensations. We walked eastward until we found the fishing boats stuck high up on the land as the tide was out. San Felipe is a kind of natural dry dock. It was a little crazy there, wandering under the big boats, all canted on their side with some about to tip over into the sand. But we went further and stripped down to out swim suits and plunged into the warm and gentle surf.

Nobody knew the history of the place and I still don't to this day. It was obviously a professional fishing village and not just a tourist trap, though tourist dollars were naturally welcome.

Later, when the sea became dark with the descent of the sun over the western range of mountains, we walked on back. I remember a cantina there, and some Mexican music happening as we had some supper. The place was really dark with few street lamps. We drifted out amongst some sheds, and with open beer bottles we bought more fish, experiencing at least one aspect of what Morrison was later to refer to as *A Feast Of Friends*.

We wandered about that town looking – for what? Remembering it now, I feel we were as much looked-at as looking.

Eventually we bought more Cerveza and drove back to the motel.

It was dark and dim there, but the sky was clear and the stars so bright; the kinds of stars you don't see anymore hanging over big American cities.

Were there signs in the heavens? Perhaps. But I did not see them nor do I think Tony saw them. If Morrison saw any he kept it to himself.

The three of us fell into deep and restful sleep.

The next day, after breakfast at the cantina, we decided that the village had been interesting as far as it went, but now it was all used up.

It was decided that we would backtrack to Mexicali, turn left and head for Tijuana, and eventually make it to the races.

Sometime later, we hit Tecate and stopped off in the town square to rest.

It was here that the trouble began.

We ate something and wandered around the square. But just as we were about to get into the car, some small Mexican kid approached with a bottle of Gold Star Tequila. We bought it for a fraction of its price and started off westward down that road, drinking it.

We got drunk, awfully fast.

What little I remember now of that wild ride comes in flashes.

I remember a bridge and a dam and what looked like a hydroelectric project. And us nipping at the bottle and getting whacked out of our skulls on that hot road.

Finally, we pulled into T.J. with its shacks and dirt streets.

We stuck to our original plan and went to the races.

I was pretty drunk by then, and all I remember of that afternoon was that in one race I bet on every single nag just to say I had come home a winner!

Then we got into the car and peeled out, with Morrison suggesting that this town was also all used up, and that we should head South to Ensenada where all the action really was.

There's a toll road and a mountain road. Naturally, we took the mountain road. More risky, more dangerous. Tony was driving. I was in back and Tony was pushing it, hitting the curves just right, and we were ripped. I mean we were really getting up there.

Then Morrison and I got into an argument.

It was over Mary.

"Hey, that chick is crazy!" he said wildly.

I wondered if he realized what he was, what we all were, there on that mountain road: out of control. But then it didn't matter. We cruised into Ensenada an poured ourselves out of the car.

Our first stop was a bar where we drank som more. I remember Tony and Jim weaving, moving in an out, but in slow motion.

Finally, we left.

We stumbled outside, down to the wharf where th boats were and where they were selling some fish in a kin of open air market. Then I remember us walking along th main drag, drunk as, well, wharf rats.

The stream of traffic moved by in spasms of ligh with Morrison weaving on ahead, until suddenly –

We were careening down a path away from all th booths and stuff above us. We were up against this sma cliff, with all these local folk streaming at our backs and wide expanse of cars below.

We were sitting on a log.

The three of us.

Alone.

And then I heard it.

I heard that voice. Oh, how I heard it! And what said, over and over again in spastic repetition, was this:

"When she comes down here, we'll leap up an snap her neck and then run down to the boats. When sh comes down here, we'll leap up and snap her neck an then run down to the boats. When she comes down here we'll leap up and snap her neck and then run down to th boats..."

Over and over again.

I looked over at Tony.

He was looking at me.

I think I was paralyzed with fear, through all tha drink.

With dread. With foreboding, I now knew some thing I had never known before about James Dougla Morrison.

I knew he could be a killer.

Tony looked at me, and I at Tony.

Tony got up and brushed by Jim and slapped him lightly on the shoulder.

I got up and said, "Time to go, Jim."

Morrison snapped awake, as if out of some nightmare, and followed us dumbly out into the crowd again. Out into that busy mound of local social life.

But what had we heard?

We climbed into Tony's Karmann Ghia again. Tony drove us down even farther South to a place he knew where there were beaches.

I felt surprisingly alive. But I had not forgotten what Jim had said on that little path by the log, that very clear, almost trance-like articulation.

We lay out there, under the glittering stars, against the soft warm Mexican sand, listening to the surf. I slept intermittently.

Then, with the dawn light, I awoke.

Tony and Jim were sprawled out at some distance from me and from each other, curled into balls and looking to me like gnarly clumps of human seaweed.

I decided not to disturb their logy dawn dreams, so I hunkered down on the beach and waited as the sun rose higher and higher.

Finally Tony stirred, unraveling and standing at the same time.

"Quite a night," I said.

"Where's Jim?" Tony asked.

"Over yonder," I said.

Jim slept on.

Tony and I walked around a bit, trying to work off our kinks and cramps.

I asked Tony if he remembered anything about Jim's monologue from the previous night, near that strip of beach.

"Man, I was scared," he said. "I knew that if some chick had wandered down there, he was going to *do it.*"

I nodded in grim affirmation. "Well, it's done-with now," I said.

I had the weird feeling that Jim had drifted out of my life.

But maybe not completely, not quite yet.

+ + +

It was following one of my long afternoons of regret and reminiscence.

The phone rang, and I picked it up.

The voice on the other end said: "Is this you, Dennis?"

"Yes"

"Wellllllll, Den," said the voice with its familiar drawl, "it's Jim."

"How do I know it's you, Jim?"

"Ask me a question. Any question," the voice slurred.

"Who's the first of the *Twelve Against the Gods*?"

"Ask Jay Sebring. He just gave me his haircut."

"How are you, Jim?"

"Fine. I just belt-whipped Nico."

"You did what? To whom?"

"Yeah. She's part of that Warhol Factory crowd ya'know. She was got up in – uh – leather. So – uh – I fucked her in the ass.

"Then, I took off my conch and belt-whipped her."

"*Goest thou to visit woman,* and do not forget to bring thy whip, eh? It's a bit literal of you to take Nietzsche that far."

"She came on to me. They all do."

"Ah, Jim... Why'd you do it?"

"Because she was a pretentious piece of shit!"

"So, if pretension is the criteria, why didn't you also belt-whip Andy?"

"Because he would've liked it, the fuck."

"So what did she feel?"

"Well, she screamed some and twisted around – uh – ya'know. And then – uh – she said a strange thing, ya'know, after it was all over. She said, 'Thanks. I needed that.' Uh – something you wrote once. I just thought I'd mention it. You're something of a prophet."

"Hmmm. Well, Jim, I don't believe in belt-whipping anyone who didn't really and truly deserve it."

"Yeah? She would've been a good woman, belt-whipped every day of her life."

"Well Jim, all I can say is, '*When the pirates count their booty they become mere thieves!*'"

Without any formality, I heard a *click* and the dial tone.

DEATH IN VENICE

I saw Morrison one last time.

Still being on good terms with Ray, I saw him during a late-afternoon sound check for a concert at the Cheetah, once again down on Venice Beach, near Pacific Ocean Park.

I remember that Ray and I talked in a friendly way, the way you might imagine old film school acquaintances would speak. Finally, Ray said, "Hey, man, Jim's out in the lobby. Why don't you try to catch him."

Jim was indeed outside in the lobby. And he was just standing there, sort of leaning, in a way that made him look like he was propped against one of the walls. I stood right in front of him with my arms crossed, not saying a word. And neither did he.

I stared at him. He would not look back. He looked harried. His face drawn. He had not yet grown fat with ease and drink.

We stayed there for a long time. How long I don't recall.

Finally, he turned away and vanished inside the club without a word and I never saw him again.

I heard from him, though.

Through Vic the painter he sent word to me to "go and see the Living Theatre. They got a performance of Frankenstein that knocks you on your ass."

Then one day in 1971, I got out of bed and as I walked past a market to get some bread, I saw the paper which said that he was dead.

AFTERMATH

I went over to the Doors office and talked to Ray and got the details, not that it mattered much by then.
    I never saw Pamela alive again, either.
    Did hear from her, one final time, over the telephone.
    I recognized her voice at once.
    "Pam" I said. "Is Jim dead?"
    There was a long silence.
    "Yeah. He's dead alright."
    Pause.
    "Say, uh, you wanna get together and smoke a number?"
    "No. I do not think a number is going to do it for me," I said.
    Then I heard the dial tone.
    Years later, when I was working on the ending of *Apocalypse Now*, I made a kind of pilgrimage to Florida in the hope of touching base with Jim's experiences there, primarily in Clearwater, where he had lived with his Grandparents while going to school. Jim had told me once about how he had set fire to the Big Cypress in his youth. He said he burned it because it was too old and too beautiful and so close to the sacred lake. A story almost certain to have been apocryphal.
    I recalled *The Temple Of The Golden Pavilion*, yet another story Jim loved.
    There, in Clearwater, I did find the "minarets" where Jim had studied his alphabet. They were perched on top of a building which was part of a college campus in that area. I never took their photograph. I've often

wondered why. I went to the place where his Grandparents lived. It had been leveled.

However, I did go to the pier on the beach at Clearwater where Jim had first met Mary. It was a pier not unlike the fishing pier back in Venice. And there was a kind of boardwalk there not unlike the boardwalk at Venice Beach. There were people milling around on the pier. And I saw a young woman there who looked almost exactly like Mary.

Mary – the survivor.

As for Pamela...

I know that perhaps some of you out there think this relationship was a tragedy.

And perhaps it was.

But consider this: Jim died in a warm bath, like an old Roman, in Paris, one of the most beautiful cities in the world. Most probably in the arms of the beautiful friend that he loved so well.

And didn't he say that he wouldn't live to be thirty?

Now where's the tragedy in this?

For, you know what the ancient Greeks used to say
Whom the Gods favour they make die young.
Call no man happy until he's dead.